D1764735

# Human Nature in the Light of Science

## Siraj Choudhury

Translated from the Bengali by
Muhammad Alamgheer and the author,
First Revised Edition in English

Ta-Ha Publishers
1 Wynne Road
London SW9 0BB
UK

Copyright © Siraj Choudhury

Published Shawwal 1421/January 2001 by:
Ta-Ha Publishers Ltd.
1 Wynne Road
London SW9 OBB
website: http://www.taha.co.uk
email: sales@taha.co.uk

By: Siraj Choudhury
Edited by: Abdassamad Clarke
General Editor: Afsar Siddiqui

British Library Cataloguing in Publication Data
Choudhury, Siraj


Human Nature and Science


I. Title

ISBN 1 84200 021 7

Typeset by: Bookwright
website: http://www.bogvaerker.dk/Bookwright
email: bookwright@bogvaerker.dk

Printed and bound by: Deluxe Printers, London NW10
Tel. : 020 8965 1771
email: de-luxe@talk21.com

# Contents

# Preface

All our efforts with our 'modernisation' and 'progressiveness' are to attain a peaceful life. In our scientific studies and our civilisation in general we are apparently progressing materially and are now seemingly much further forward in that sense. But tranquillity – actual peace and tranquillity – we cannot find anywhere, because man cannot find his own true nature. He does not know that tranquillity and peace are in his own nature. All creatures, except some men, know their own natures and they thus have peace within their own natures. If the natural world was unpeaceful, there would have been a dreadful disaster in human society. Even man as a species would have perished and perhaps might still do so.

Now – "nature". What is the meaning of this word "nature". In Arabic it is the word *fitrah*, which means that each creature has been created on its own innate form with its natural duty to fulfil. So the actual meaning is a creature's natural condition. Now, what is the meaning of the term natural condition? Take, for instance, the sun: if it is not able to shine onto the earth it does not fulfil its natural condition, and what would then happen to the earth? That so-called sun would not be regarded as a sun, because its nature would not be as it should be. Similarly, if every kind of creature did not fulfil its natural condition, properly and promptly, the world would be a place of disaster, and all creatures would cease to exist. Without the natural condition, or "nature", no creatures would exist. This is a scientific truth. For example, the nature of fruit consists in the taste and goodness within it. The nature of something forbidden consists of the badness within it.

So the nature, or natural duty of a creature is its religion, which in Arabic is called *deen*. Deen is nothing else but nature. This means that the deen of any creature is its own nature. Now, let us take man. Man is not apart from the world of nature. So what is the nature of man? What is his natural duty? To eat, drink and live socially is not the meaning of his nature. Even animals live in such a fashion. In other words, as man is the supreme creature, his nature should be above that of all the other creatures. Today, there is no peace or tranquillity for man or human society. And the sole reason for this is that man is not acting according to his nature, he is not fulfilling his natural duty.

The natural duty of every kind of creature is its deen. But men are not fulfilling their natural duty. They are not acting in accordance with their own natures. Men have so many religions, but that is to say so many natures. This is unwise, uncivilised and unscientific for the supreme creature. This is why we see enmity, wars and battles, because of the different religions in human society. All human beings should have one nature, their natural duty, the same for every human being. Otherwise men will have no nature, or will have an evil nature, an inhuman nature.

Today, perhaps we call search in the light of science, and will be able to find out the actual nature of human beings and their natural duties, so that peace and prosperity may be found.

I would like to express my gratitude to Sheikh Zahurul Haque Choudhury, Doctor Samiak, Sheikh Muhammad Hanif, Asad bin Hafiz, W. T. Acton, and British TV personality and writer Tim Rifat. Without their help it would not have been possible to publish this book.

Siraj Choudhury

# What Religion connotes

"**A** precise definition of the term religion is difficult indeed. Numerically, territorially and politically religion has different shades and substances. But however it does not mean that we should throw up our hands in despair and abandon our search for the basic grounds of the various faiths and their various distinctive characteristics or traits."

To this distinguished philosopher religion has three phases; viz. Faith, Thought and Discovery. Faith means belief in a Supreme-Being, without rhyme or reason; Thought refers to the realisation of that Being with rational understanding of it, and Discovery implies the finding out of practicable ways of making contact with that Supreme-Being.

Human belief, he felt, was in that primary stage of religion an all-pervading paganism, at a time when human life was enormously simple and needs were limited. As a result people could easily satisfy their basic needs with whatever they had within reach. In leisure, they felt an urge to know the vast universe with its many wonders, like mountains, rivers, clouds, the sun and the stars in the sky, etc. All these cravings led them to the way of primitive paganism, consisting in rituals, offering worship to such wonders.

That is the standard explanation of western 'comparative religion'. Muslims know that all men from the beginning of time have received revelations through their prophets who guided them to knowledge of the Divine and worship of Him, and that these pure revelations of tawhid – knowledge of the Oneness of Allah – degenerated through time and forgetfulness into later polytheisms and corrupted religions.

Comparative religion's explanation continues that following primitive paganism, the early peoples, with the march of time, gradually developed Taoism but this is not true, because Taoism is concerned with the dynamic interplay of opposites within the Taoist vision of Unity. It is probably the decadence of an ancient prophetic revelation. Similarly, Confucianism which dwells on good government and administration may be the remnants of an ancient shari'ah. Then Buddhism offers man salvation through the abandonment of his desires and extinction of 'self', and is in reality an effort to reform the various teachings found in India and known today as Hinduism.

Hinduism also made its appearance in the guise of religion. It is a religion parts of which were innovated by the people of different ages and times. According to Gupta the term 'Hindu' is of foreign origin. In Arabic, 'Hind' is the name of the country India, and Hinduism is therefore the collection of creeds and practices to be found there, which may well be degenerations of ancient revelations.

Some other religions do not suffer from such obscurity especially regarding their origins and foundations. Among these are Christianity, Judaism and Islam. All these are based on revelations and the prophets to whom they were revealed.

Deen, in a true sense, should be capable of tending to the all-round welfare of mankind, or else it is not, by any means, deen. It is not a mere faith stuffed with stories resembling fairy tales to be enjoyed in a romantic manner, and the man who thinks so is either a bigot, or an idiot living in society to undo the peace and progress of the people and the surrounding world.

Nowadays man is seen selfishly and heartlessly becoming materialist. He puts his trust in external material reality. The stories of sacred books have little appeal for him. As a result, atheism has appeared on the earth. If deen is for man, it ought to be a single one, letting no room exist for the growth of many other creeds or faiths, because many of the rites and rituals of many religions tend to mar and stain humanity and civilisation. Such growth now operates in our life and society, with the endurance of many ancient and now decadent creeds and the appearance of many new ones.

The intention here is not to hurt nor undermine any particular religion. No religion belongs exclusively to any particular people or group, and thus any talk or criticism of any Creed or Faith should offer no opportunity for creating friction and quarrels among any rival groups. There is no intention here to imply that any particular religion is either a true or untrue one, rather, to believe that all religions were originally for the welfare of mankind, though they multiply the methods of ritual, this or that way, in our life. It is accepted by convention that religion should have all the traits and qualities to solve the problems ever permeating human life, and that one must be committed to being peaceful in oneself and comforting to others. Otherwise what is the utility of religion in human life and why should it be followed?

Here a humble endeavour is made to discuss some issues to let us genuinely try to comprehend the worth of life, freed from anxieties, the life that can let us realise peace and happiness in reality and truth, in the content and context, of course, of the Divine Code that guarantees such realisation.

# The Creator: In Realisation?

Who made the vast universe and all that exists within it? This question arises in man's mind. And man thinks himself capable of answering it. The people who failed yesterday to give a satisfactory answer to this question, now seem to answer it today. The more science marches ahead, the clearer and more convincing its answers become to man, but it never even approaches answering this question. Man believes in that which is not visible, or cannot be perceived by the five sense organs, has no immediately apparent physical existence and hence can command no faith in the human mind, though its actions are seen reflected at every moment, realised and even sometimes conspicuously felt: I am talking about oxygen! In this context, how should man then conceptualise He Who is not visible? It is science that teaches us to believe in His sublime being, if we really think correctly.

In our self exists the heart, that we call soul, which we feel obscurely, when it creates indiscernible ripples in the ocean of our feelings and emotions, making us move and recognise our existence. To remove its impact from our thoughts and intellects means to make us mere physical matter, turning us into spiritual cyphers, mere nothingnesses. It is because of this that our being in life rests wholly on the soul — the self that keenly compels us to put belief in Him, the Invisible Divinity. To make it more clear, we experience that on this mortal earth human life is ultimately limited by inevitable death. This soul of mine is part of a Great Infinity. Being bounded by its material cage the body, however, fails to recognise the self unless it aspires to be acquainted with that being. Man is physically a creature made up of flesh and blood and as such his life tends to torture his soul or self by doing wrong.

People of the 21st century utilise such influences to delude man by indoctrinating him with the belief that the vast universe is self-made, and hence has no creator with Whom we should keep faith and reflect upon.

Man observes the universe in two ways: one with his physical eyesight, the other with his mind, or insight. This way he tries to realise 'self' and the 'world'. If he fails to employ either of these sights in studying life and the world, he becomes a one-eyed half-blind man. He sees, for instance, only the boat that he has boarded, but fails to think about the maker of the boat. As a result, such a man commits the same blunder regarding the Creator of the vast universe in which he lives. Such a type of man is out-and-out insane or stupid, living worthlessly on earth.

Man knows that the vast universe is not of his own creating. The luminous sky, the green earth with its various features such as its mountains, oceans, deserts, etc., – all these exhibit to man a unique beauty, discipline and system which evoke an awe in him, in his soul. All these show us that the universe is an absolutely perfect creation in the upkeep and administration of its own laws. Man has made no contribution to its creation, nor has he any sort of power of any degree or nature to do or undo this system. Such thinking makes man bewildered, awed and confounded!

Again it is a proven fact that man can create many wonders on earth. He can fly to the moon, dive into the fathomless bottom of the ocean, destroy a vast tract of land by simply switching an electric button and so on and so forth. It appears that man now possesses more than a giant's strength to dictate his will over earth, without facing any resistance or obstacle. He has almost become the master of nature, in such a way that the latter, it seems, has now become a slave to serve his sweet will and wishes, except that nature is apparently paying him back with the death of the oceans and the biosphere and the death of man's own heart. In other words, modern man feels that the entire creation is, more or less, at his disposal and discretion, forced to abide by his orders to please him, in all ways possible.

By contrast, it is to be noted that this mighty man is very often unable to chase away even an infection-bearing fly. He becomes quite helpless in facing natural calamities like cyclones, earthquakes, floods and droughts, etc. He is so helpless that he cannot even calm a little squall for the sake of his peace of mind, and for the tranquillity of his environment! Why does it happen so? It is because mighty man, although well-armoured with macro- and micro-science and technology, has no power to dictate *nature's* will, the will that is beyond his control and petty conceptions.

Again, water and food are essential for the sustenance of life. Clouds and rain regularly provide us with the essential life-sustaining and invigorating elements. Wind is also at work to fulfil our needs: it carries water-vapour, causing rain to fall on different parts of the earth. Man has no role here. Similarly no human power can be accredited with the process of childbirth, nor can man, by the force of his will, make the baby in the womb of its mother to be born either as a male or female. The kingdom of the heavens is also free from human-control. Luminous bodies like the sun, the moon and stars, the immense planets, known and unknown, are constantly rotating and orbiting at tremendous speed, without the least deviation from their routes, because of a great and surprisingly vast discipline which has been existing in the sky from time immemorial. All these that we chance upon, every now and then, certainly do follow some order prescribed and ordained by some Great One, and that One alone.

Atheists do not acknowledge the existence of the Creator of these creations. They stress matter and reasoning, reality and perception as the criteria for judging truths and beliefs. Things that are perceptible to the senses, and, of course, visible from the viewpoint of science, are to them to be treated as facts and realities, and such things and matters should be the basis of any Faith or Creed. Beyond reasoning, that is beyond the perception and reality perceived by the five senses, there is nothing to consider or imagine as truth or reality. Atheists are seen relentlessly working to project such a concept of life and the universe into the kingdoms of our thought and intellect. To their grammar of speculation, the existence of the Divine Entity is an element foreign to human thought.

Let us now look into the natures and actions of animals. They are endowed with life, strength, and the ability to experience feelings of pain and pleasure. A wild tiger roars when it is angry, stealthily proceeds to hunt when it feels hunger, and is seen wagging its tail at time of rest or licking its body. Or a pet animal, a dog or a cat say, exhibits loyalty to its master and follows all his commands. These examples show us the animals believing, or more or less having faith in the things which are visible, perceptible and which are able to arouse feelings in them. In this regard man is quite identical with lower animals in eating, drinking, copulating, and in feeling happiness and sorrow. Yet, on close observation one can see that animals too have an awareness of the unseen, and that they praise their Creator, as Allah tells us in Qur'an.

Atheists are here right in stating the axiomatic proposition "Man is a rational animal" – a primary statement of their logic. And here man and animals are almost 100 percent equal in their actions and way of life. Then where lies the distinction between these two species? Why is man regarded as superior to animals? Humans have some properties that are absent in animals. These are mind, consciousness of self, and soul which have endowed him with the ability to judge what is good and beneficial and what is detrimental to self and other creatures. He can think, feel, dream, and remember, and he can exercise free-will to choose between right or wrong. But an animal has no such faculty of mind and intellect. That means a man can educate himself, enlighten his mind and regulate his manner and disposition. An animal cannot. Inquisitiveness is another salient feature with him.

In the Glorious Qur'an Allah says: **"Because of that We showed Ibrahim the dominions of the heavens and the earth so that he might be one of the people of certainty."**

Finally observing their fleeting movement and departure he concludes his queries by saying:

**"Then when it set he said, 'My people, I am free of what you associate**

with Allah! I have turned my face to Him Who brought the heavens and earth into being, a pure natural believer. I am not one of the mushrikun.'"

The last and final Prophet of Islam, i.e. for mankind, the Prophet Muhammad (SAAS) received his Prophethood after much questionings about the self, his society and the people of his time and country. The cave of Hira was his abode in which he received the Divine light of Heaven. It occurred when the Messenger Angel Jibril (AS) appeared and taught him to say '*IQRA*' i.e. **"Recite: In the Name of your Lord who created, created man from clots of blood. Recite: And your Lord is the Most Generous, He who taught by the pen, taught man what he did not know."** (Surah 96:1-5)

These are some of the ever-living, ever-shining examples of man's inborn urge to satisfy his inquisitiveness of mind and soul that always inspire him to know his Creator through His awe-inspiringly vast creation of the universe! The people who are on the right track of thinking are divinely fortunate because they receive right knowledge about their Lord and wisdom, and, conversely, those who are unfortunate go astray in disobeying their conscience's dictates.

# Man is Immortal

As we were once born so we will die; this is the plain truth on which we can all agree. No matter how great or how mighty we are, we will have to die when it is time. Men, so busy with their daily lives, are little aware of the passing of a year. Days, months and years pass so speedily. This brief life ends one day. No matter how much money you spend to prolong it, you cannot save your life when it's time to die.

Not many people today believe that there is eternal life after death, because we do not have any practical proof of that life. Nobody comes back from the dead to tell us about the life hereafter. Only revelation tells us about that eternal life. But which revelation is to be trusted? It is the revelation of the deen which is shown to be the only true deen by the Creator of the universe; the deen which is proved in every way scientifically and experientially, both practically and theoretically; the deen with a complete code of life, must be the only true deen for man. If there is One Creator or God there can be only one deen. Several deens mean several Gods, and this is unscientific and not acceptable to civilised people.

My 'self' does not mean my body. My 'self' means my soul, which is the main or original 'self'. If there is no soul that means there is no being. The body alone does not constitute man's existence on earth. The soul is the main and original being, and when that goes out of the body there is no being. Man has died, or left this earth, and his body remains, to vanish in soil and dust. So the body alone is not existence for man. The main 'myself' is invisible. We cannot see it, but we are aware when it departs, and when it goes, the man concerned no longer exists on the earth. So this is the plain truth: man is immortal, man does not die, he only leaves the body, and goes elsewhere.

But where does he go to? Of course he goes to another place, but we must consider what his existence would be like there. It would, of course, be a consequence of his actions in this life: evil deeds leading to punishment and good deeds leading to peace and happiness. Every action has its reaction: this is the plain truth. So every action in this life will have its consequences in the life hereafter. There are two principal events in our life: birth and death. Death is actually another birth. Birth and death are not 'beginning' and 'end', birth and death are changes of position and place.

Islam says that man is born on this earth from his mother's womb, with a child's body, and that he will be born from this earth with a youth's body on Doom's Day. In the interim, after so-called death, until Doom's Day, there is an existence of dreams and sleep, in a place which is called *'Alam al-Barzakh* – the world of the interspace.

From our births as children from our mothers' wombs this Earth is our place for learning, to gain the knowledge of our rank as human beings. According to the knowledge gained we lead our lives on the right path or the wrong path. This is our test of humanity; whether we pass or fail we will know the final result on Doom's Day, or the Final Day of Judgement. To get the final result whether good or bad, we will then be reborn on Doom's Day, or the Day of Rising, from the womb of the earth, with youthfulness, but maturity, to see, feel and suffer the consequences. So the superiority of human beings is to be prosperous in every way, and everywhere, here and hereafter, and that is in accordance with our actions in this life, but if our actions are evil it is to be miserable hereafter forever.

# Islam and other Creeds

The 'Code of Life' revealed by the Creator is absolutely perfect, and capable of guiding humans in every possible way. It is the sole panacea for all human ills and problems, ranging from individual life to global life, in any and every aspect. Any code which failed to render such a service to mankind, in any degree or form, could not be treated as guidance from Heaven.

Secondly, the code should be for all, irrespective of their race, creed – and indeed Islam alone has a revealed code allowing for dwelling with followers of other religions under the shari'ah[1] – colour and status. It should also have provision for the welfare of other creatures. All have their rights and dues in the eyes of the Lord's law and no one can escape from it. Unlike the Hindu's caste system, it should guarantee the honour and status of each man, whatever might be his rank or blood. Contrary to the ascendancy of the Papacy in Roman Catholicism and the various orthodox churches with their Patriarchs, it should give the freedom for all to go to their prayer-houses, to perform their rituals, unfettered, unmolested and un-persecuted.

Hence the code, or such convictions regarding the Creator and the deen, is not a property to be inherited by a priestly class, or by blood or by ascendancy. The only measure of his deen for any man is his *taqwa*[2] and iman[3] and fear of Allah, that is his firm devotion to the worship of Allah, the Almighty. Worship here includes all thoughts, words and deeds that are reflected in the contents of prayer, remembrance, fasting, and generosity in sadaqah, etc., offered in or out of the mosque, where the prayer-house assumes the life-role of being the focus of a human being's activities, from his birth to

---

[1, 2, 3] See the footnotes on page 24, and also see the Glossary on page 88

the grave. Hence it means deen is not only a personal matter to be kept confined to the abode of prayer alone, nor it is one's personal choice to be followed to suit one's own sweet will, rather it is a unique practice to be shared, practised and implemented by each and every sane man and woman, for reforming the mind and manner of mankind both individually and collectively. Any deviation in this regard must be corrected, to save the people and the world we live in from deeds, words and even thoughts which are counter to the deen of Allah.

In this context let us now examine the beliefs and activities of the leaders of three of the major living religions: Islam, Christianity and Hinduism.

1. ISLAM. Islam in its final and comprehensive form came into full existence with its last and greatest Prophet, Muhammad (SAAS), after all the glorious civilisations of the ancient world – the Indian, Chinese, Persian, Greek, and Egyptian – had already reached the nadir of their decline. It is, therefore, universally accepted that Islam alone presents the perfect concept of deen as the code of life revealed to mankind from time to time ever since the appearance of man on this earth. It contains clear and complete guidance concerning both the spiritual and material aspects of human life. With such divine qualities and elements, it has a profound influence upon other religions of the world. It has had the unique distinction of winning the hearts of people who, being fortified with courage, strength and determination, struggle in life to spread the light and benefits of Islam throughout the globe. This is the foremost and final deen of the world, as stated in the last and final revealed Book: the Glorious Qur'an. It is not confined to rites and rituals, to be performed and followed by its followers, alone. Rather it is a complete code, embracing both the individual and the collective lives – indeed global life – of mankind.

As it belongs to each and every one, no single man or authority has any monopoly over this creed. Consequently in Islam there is no priesthood, nor any hereditary system to be taken into account and offering religious ascendancy and status to any one. The spiritual and moral leadership of it only goes to that individual who is superior to others in respect of taqwa, honesty, and sacrifice, from the viewpoint of the sacred Book, the Qur'an. In addition, there is full scope for others to dauntlessly criticise even leading figures if their deeds and words are found to violate the injunctions and the limits of Islam. Not only this, any member of the ummah has the full-right to exert and exercise his will against such a leader to the extent of bringing him before a qadi for fair trial and judgement in matters of personal dispute. In these matters, even the ruler is only one of the muslims. Moreover, the muslims have a right to depose leaders who have clearly embraced kufr. This is because man is imperfect and subject to error, except the final Prophet, Muhammad (SAAS)

In Islam, it is recommended that the man who is superior in following and practising the Qur'anic directives, both in word and deed, and who is gifted with the ability to lead men in war and peace, is to be given the authority of governing the community. And hence it is apparent that the best man in terms of the deen in the society might be the head of the community, as has happened throughout Islamic history, and his activities would not be confined to the prayer-house, as his mere personal affairs, rather they would also be the model for the people to inspire them to improve their characters and dealings. For instance, the Caliph 'Umar (RA), the Prophet Mohammed's (SAAS) companion, was seen in the mosque being accused by an ordinary citizen because of two pieces of clothing he had put on that day. When the Caliph made it clear that his son had given him his clothing for his use and that he owned only two pieces, the complainant became happy, and thereafter the Caliph delivered his *khutbah* (address delivered by the imam who leads the Friday prayer) in the mosque. This is the true and genuine picture of the leader of Islam, the leader who, in his taqwa, used to lead both politically and in acts of worship because of his unstained character and deeds.

2. CHRISTIANITY. Now let us have a look into Christianity and the papacy of the Roman Catholic branch, which after its annihilation of other more authentic forms and before Martin Luther's age (1483–1546) was

almost the only form of Christianity in Europe. In the true sense, the deen of the Prophet 'Isa (AS), called Jesus in the English version of the Bible, was not named Christianity. His later adherents followed the Bible according to their own sweet wills, and so they utterly failed to have iman in him as their Prophet. They took him as the son of the Virgin Maryam, called Mary in the Bible. With devilish reasoning and thought, they presented their prophet as the son of God and innovated the doctrine of the trinity – i.e. God the father, 'Isa the son, and the Holy Ghost or Spirit (although sometimes it is unclear as to whether or not Mary is a fourth). On that concept and faith they began to practise in such a way that some of them developed monasticism in their society and life. Splitting the unity of society between church and state they introduced the system of creating priests to conduct rites and rituals among the people in their churches. However, state and church were actually intimately joined, as the church was merely a way for the Roman state to endure. To maintain their authority, the priests made the Biblical teaching their property and asset, and in society they administered rites and rituals on behalf of God for the redemption of the mass of the people who were in a permanent condition of being accused of doing wrong and of sinning. Corporal punishment, sometimes accompanied by a monetary penalty, was imposed on the layman for penance. As the public were brutally and dexterously kept ignorant of Scripture, the church had the arbitrary power to guide, control, and punish sinners! – awarding even the death penalty to mitigate the wrath of the Lord, the holy Father of the universe.

From this brief sketch, it is quite clear that Roman Christianity has made the Papacy an unchallengeable power over people in conducting their religious lives. Not only this. State authority had also been made subject to their command to settle theocratic issues affecting state laws and administration. Joan of Arc was, for example, condemned to be burnt to death for sorcery by this unbridled Papal system of Roman Christianity.

3. HINDUISM. Unlike Islam, Christianity or Judaism, Hinduism has no revealed book to be followed by its people. The late Pandit Jawher lal Nehru was of the opinion that 'Hinduism' is not a religion at all; it is rather a

bundle of beliefs deduced from the *Ramayana* and *Mahabharata* – the epics made by two genii. In his book *The Discovery of India* Nehru expresses his opinion regarding Hinduism in the following words:

"Hinduism as a faith is vague, amorphous, manysided, all things to all men. It is hardly possible to define it, or indeed to say definitely whether it is religion or not, in the usual sense of the term… It embraces many beliefs and practices, from the highest to the lowest, often opposed to, or contradicting, each other." (p37)

That means Hinduism cannot claim the same status and value which other religions based on sacred revealed scriptures enjoy.

Secondly, the obnoxious caste system of the Hindus is sheer degradation for a great number of people. Save the Brahmins and the Khatriyas – the two highly and strangely built-up privileged classes – the rest are treated as non-humans who have been sent to earth as slaves to unquestioningly serve privileged people who may command without rhyme or reason. Mahatma Gandhi's feeble movement for raising the status of the Harijan – the despised lowest caste – is a glaring example of the trampling down of humanity in the name and guise of so-called religion. Like the Jews of Isra'il, the present Indian privileged classes consider themselves the destined and chosen people of God, sent to rule, and not to be ruled, on earth. The Brahmins, the guardians of the Hindu religion, believe themselves to be lords over the Sudra and Vaisya castes (the lowest Hindu castes). To suit their own desires, the lives and existences of these two classes are entrusted to them – i.e. the Brahmins and the Khatriyas – and they have arbitrary powers. They are considered super-beings because they never commit sins or do any wrong at any time.

The Khatriyas – the rulers of the state – act as the collaborators of the Brahmins in keeping the downtrodden castes always loyal and submissive to the Brahmins' orders and injunctions.

Thus it can be seen that all other religions, including Hinduism, are designed and practised to safeguard the vested interests of a group of people, in such a way that commoners feel it better for them to obey their lords, rather than, with their poor status and poverty, to rebel against those lords.

4. JUDAISM. A few words on Judaism would not be redundant here. It had, like Christianity or Islam, scriptures, prophets and apostles. The *Torah* and its messenger Musa (AS) – called Moses in the Bible – show that the Children of Israel were worshippers of one God only, and were asked to follow their Prophet with true hearts and dedication. But this community, with a few exceptions, went astray. The so-called leaders of their community tampered with the *Torah* and misled the people into disobeying Musa (AS) considering him a nonsensical preacher of faith. For this act of kufr and disobedience they were cursed by Allah Himself, both here and in the hereafter.

Judaism, according to the *Encyclopaedia of Religion and Ethics*, is a scar upon the faith of its followers :

"A formal and precise definition of Judaism is a matter of some difficulty, because it raises the question what is the absolute and irreducible minimum of conformity? ... the foundation of Judaism rests on two principles, the unity of God and the choice of Israel. It believes in a universal God, but it is not exclusive." [Vol.8, p581]

This accursed usury-practising community has now become jingoistic and, with the practice of Zionism, have become vindictive against the peoples of the world, politically, economically and even in the guise of missionary activities.

## Christianity versus Judaism and Islam
It was during either the month of Rajab or Sha'ban (two months of the Islamic calendar immediately preceding Ramadan) of the 2nd year hijri[1],

---

[1] Hijri: a year in the Islamic calendar, which started from the year when the Prophet Muhammad (SAAS) and his companions emigrated from Makkah to Madinah.

that Allah in the sacred Qur'an commanded the Prophet Muhammad (SAAS) and his followers to turn their faces from Bait al-Muqaddas in Jerusalem to the Ka'bah in Makkah. The Jews instantly and vividly understood that the Prophet Muhammad (SAAS) is the last and final Prophet of Islam and the successor of all the prophets who had earlier been sent to each nation to show Islam and the message of the coming of Muhammad (SAAS) as the final Messenger of Allah to complete their missions. But neither the Jews nor the Christians of his time accepted him as Allah's last Messenger, though both had been the owners of scriptures and used to undermine each other every now and then on the question of their respective superiority in respect of their faiths. In the words of the Glorious Qur'an:

"The Jews say, 'The Christians have nothing to stand on,' and the Christians say, 'The Jews have nothing to stand on,' yet they both recite the Book." (Surat al-Baqarah 2:112)

Hence it is apparent that they are misled by their vanity and vested interests and hence Allah says to His Messenger Muhammad (SAAS):

"We have sent you with the Truth, bringing good news and giving warning. Do not ask about the inhabitants of the Blazing Fire. The Jews and the Christians will never be pleased with you until you follow their religion. Say, 'Allah's guidance is the true guidance.' If you were to follow their whims and desires, after the knowledge that has come to you, you would find no protector or helper against Allah. " (Surah 2: 119-120)

Instead of coming into the fold of the Islam being taught by Muhammad (SAAS) the Christians instituted 'Isa (AS) as the son of God, whereas the Jews slandered him (may Allah save the Muslims from such conduct).

Similarly the *Vedas-Puran* and *Upanishads* of the Hindus, *Digha Nikaya* of the Buddhists, *Jinda Besta* and *Dushati* of the Persians prophesied the appearance of the Prophet Muhammad (SAAS) as the last and greatest Messenger of Allah and admonished that he should be followed, and his teachings obeyed, wholeheartedly and with dedication. But alas! – unfortunately, they were also unable to see the true light which is a gift for all mankind for them to enjoy a joyous life here in this world, and to attain eternal peace and pleasure in the hereafter!

The Book – the Noble Qur'an – with its proven Messenger, forever the only perfect man on earth, was thus wickedly and contemptuously belittled by the ungrateful, both in mind and manner, deed and word!

Islam is the single unique guidance from Heaven revealed to mankind through the train of its messengers – the Prophets and Messenger, Muhammad (SAAS) being the last of this line. They were all teachers to teach mankind Islam both in letter and spirit, thought and reality.

### Conclusion
Thus the teaching of the Prophets of Islam have made man aware of his relation with his:

1.　Creator – the Lord and Sustainer of the universe,

2.　Surroundings – nature and all other creations,

3.　His own self – concerning his being, Creator and surroundings.

It is by their noble deeds and sacrifices that the true civilisation of the world has flourished by degrees, the Prophet Muhammad (SAAS) being its zenith.

### What the Bible says about Islam and Muhammad (SAAS):
Here are some examples from the Bible[1]. History has shown that the Bible suffered changes throughout the ages. Despite these changes there are still some chapters containing words telling of Islam and the Prophet Muhammad (SAAS) as the final Messenger of Allah, and Islam as the only true deen from Allah.

---

1. The Bible in general is divided into two main parts: the 'Old Testament' which was written before the advent of 'Isa (AS) sometime after the return of the Children of Israel from Babylonian captivity (after 536 BCE), and the 'New Testament' which was written long after the departure of 'Isa (AS) and describes his life and teachings, and the activities of his disciples and apostles in spreading the Christian religion.

"For I am God, and there is none else; I am God and there is none like me." Isaiah, 46

Yes, God is one and there is none like him. As Allah says in the Noble Qur'an – Surah 112:

**"Say: He is Allah, Absolute Oneness, Allah, the Everlasting Sustainer of all. He has not given birth and was not born. And no one is comparable to Him."**

"The prophet which prophesieth of peace, when the word of the prophet shall come to pass, then shall the prophet be known, that the Lord has truly sent him." Jeremiah, 28:9

Does this not apply to Muhammad (SAAS)? The word 'Islam' signifies submission and stems from a root meaning tranquillity and peace, peace between the Lord Creator and His creations. This prophecy of Jeremiah cannot be applied to 'Isa (AS) or any other person, as 'Isa himself stated that he did not come for peace.

"Suppose ye that I am come to give peace on earth? I tell you, Nay, but rather division: for from henceforth there will be five in one house divided, three against two and two against three. The father shall be divided against the son, and the son against the father; the mother against the daughter, and the daughter against the mother; the mother-in-law against the daughter-in-law, and the daughter-in-law against the mother-in-law". Luke, 12:51-53

" And I will pray to the father, and he shall give you another Comforter, that he shall abide with you for ever." John, 14:16

Let us examine, in the light of the Bible, if this Comforter fits the character of the Prophet Muhammad (SAAS):

"Another Comforter" means that many Comforters had come, and another one was to come.

"...that he shall abide with you for ever" means that there was no need for another Comforter to come after him, and he was the completion of all the prophets. His teaching will abide, and for ever remain intact. In fact, the Noble Qur'an and all his teachings remain as they were over 1400 years ago.

"Howbeit when he, the spirit of truth is come, he will guide you into all truth; for he shall not speak of himself; but whatsoever he shall hear, that shall he speak; and he will show things to come." John, 16:13

"The spirit of truth" – the Prophet Muhammad (SAAS) was called *al-Ameen* (the honest or trustworthy one) since his childhood.

"...for he shall not speak of himself; but whatsoever he shall hear, that shall he speak" – the noble Qur'an is Allah's speech. There is not a single word included from the Prophet Muhammad (SAAS) or his companions. The angel Jibril (AS) read it to him, he memorised it, and it was written down by his scribes. His own sayings were recorded in *Hadith*, or Tradition.

"...and will put my words in his mouth; and he shall speak unto them all that I shall command him." Deuteronomy, 18:18

This corresponds with Surah 53: 2-4 of the noble Qur'an: "**Your companion [Muhammad (SAAS)] is not misguided or misled; nor does he speak from whim. It is nothing but Revelation revealed.**"

"And the book is delivered to him that is not learned, saying, read this, I pray thee and he saith, I am not learned." Isaiah, 29:12

The first revelation of Allah through the Angel Jibril (AS) to Muhammad (SAAS) was the word *IQRA'* which means 'Read-recite', in Surah 96:1-5 of the noble Qur'an. As he was unlettered he replied, 'I cannot read'. The revelations did not occur in the same order in which they appear in the Noble Qur'an. In other words the first revelation is not on the first page, and the final revelation is not on the last page. The revelations came in instalments and were inserted in a certain order in the Qur'an as ordained by Allah and as the Prophet (SAAS) commanded the writers. That is also mentioned in the Bible:

> "For precept must be upon precept, precept upon precept, line upon line, line upon line; here a little and there a little: for with stammering lips and another tongue will he speak to his people." Isaiah, 28:10-11

Another tongue means here another language, not Hebrew or Aramaic, but Arabic. Muslims all over the world use this language in calling on Allah, in their prayers, in pilgrimage and in greeting each other. This unity of language had also been prophesied in the Bible:

> "For then will I turn to the people a pure language, that they may all call upon the name of the Lord, serve him with one consent." Zephaniah, 3:9

> "And it shall come to pass that whosoever will not hearken unto my words which he shall speak in My name, I will require it of him." Deuteronomy 18:19

In the noble Qur'an all but one of the Surahs (chapters) start with, "In the name of Allah, most Gracious, most Merciful." Muslims in their daily work also start with this saying. Not in the name of God or Lord, but "in My name", God's own name – Allah. As it is God's personal name, it does not imply gender as does God or Goddess. Christians start with, "In the name of the Father, the Son and the Holy Spirit." In fact, whose name is taken is not clear.

It is to be noted that those who will not hear him, or will deny him, will be punished. As in the noble Qur'an (Surah 3:19) Allah says, **"The deen with Allah is Islam."** And in Surah 3: 84, **"If anyone desires anything other than Islam as a deen, it will not be accepted from him, and in the akhirah[1] he will be among the losers."**

> "Therefore thy gates shall be open continually; they shall not be shut

---

[1] See the Glossary on page 88.

day or night, that men may bring unto thee the forces of the Gentiles, and their Kings may be brought." Isaiah, 60

It is clearly a fact that the mosque surrounding the sacred Ka'bah (House of Allah) in Makkah has remained open day and night since it was cleansed by the Prophet Muhammad (SAAS) of idols over 1400 years ago. Rulers, as well as subjects, from all over the world come annually, and all the year round, for pilgrimage. No church or any other house of worship, not even the Vatican, remains open day and night, except this house of Allah in Makkah.

"And this is the record of John (Yahya), when Jews sent priests and laity from Jerusalem to ask him, who art thou? And he confessed and denied not, but confessed – I am not the Christ. And they asked him, What then? Art thou Elias? And he saith I am not. Art thou that prophet? And he answered no. And they asked him and said unto him, why baptisest thou them, if thou be not the Christ, nor Elias, neither that prophet? John answered them, saying, I baptize with water, but there standeth one amongst you, who ye know not. He it is who coming after me is preferred before me, whose shoes' latchet I am not worthy to unloose." St. John, 1:19-27

Now the crucial question is – "Art thou *that* prophet?" Who was then *that* long-awaited prophet after 'Isa and Yahya (John) (AS)? Was he not the prophet Muhammad (SAAS)? Can Judaeo-Christians answer this question? The answer is – yes, Muhammad (SAAS) is indeed "*that* prophet".

The Tawrah (*Torah*) was revealed to the Prophet Musa (AS). To prove the veracity of one of the verses from the *Torah* the distinguished religious writer, Rev. James L. Dow, wrote in his *Dictionary of the Bible*:

"The only man of history who can be compared even remotely to him (Moses) is Mahomet (Muhammad)."

---

1. See *The Miracle of the Qur'an* on page 56.

Here is a verse from the Persian *Jinda Besta* about Muhammad (SAAS) AS the last and most supreme Messenger of Allah:

*"Noid te 'Ahmad'* (Muhammad's second name) *dragoyeitim flam-raomi. Spetame Zurathustra yam dahmam vangnim afritim. Yunad hake hahi humananghad havakanghad Hushyanthnad hudaenad."* i.e.:

"I am announcing, O Spetame Zurathustra, the holy Ahmad will surely come, from whom you will get the thought of the truths, speak of the truths and the true and clean religion."

So what more would a man need to know to prove the truthfulness and authenticity of a religion? In other words the Miracle of Miracles, the Noble Qur'an[1] and the beauties of Islam are the adequate living proof to man, for over 1,400 years.

### The Message of Islam

The message of Islam is revealed to all prophets, because Islam is for all mankind. In the Noble Qur'an Allah says to all:

**"Say, 'We have iman in Allah and what has been sent down to us and what was sent down to Ibrahim, Isma'il and Ishaq and Ya'qub and the Tribes, and what Musa and 'Isa and all the Prophets were given by their Lord. We do not differentiate between any of them. We are Muslims submitted to Him.' If anyone desires anything other than Islam**

---

[1] The Muslim position is very clear. The Muslim does not claim to have a deen peculiar to himself. Islam is not a sect or an ethnic religion. In its view all deen is one, for the truth is one. It is the deen which was taught by all the prophets. It is the truth taught by all the revealed Books. In essence it amounts to a consciousness of the will and plan of Allah and a joyful submission to that will and plan. If anyone wants a deen other than that, he is false to his own nature, as he is false to Allah's will and plan. Such a one cannot expect guidance, for he has deliberately renounced guidance.

as a deen, it will not be accepted from him, and in the akhirah he will be among the losers."[1] (Surah Al 'Imran: 84-85)

"You who have iman! have taqwa[2] of Allah[3] with the taqwa due to Him and do not die except as Muslims (with complete submission to Allah)." (Surah Al 'Imran: 102-3)

---

[2] An element of taqwa is fear. Fear is of many kinds: 1) the abject fear of a coward; 2) the fear of a child or an inexperienced person in the face of an unknown danger; 3) the fear of a reasonable man who wishes to avoid harm to himself or to people whom he wishes to protect; 4) the reverence which is akin to love, for it fears to do anything which is not pleasing to the object of love.

The first is unworthy of man, the second is necessary for one immature, the third is a manly precaution against evil as long as it is unconquered, and the fourth is the seedbed of right-action. Those mature in iman cultivate the fourth; the third or the second may be necessary, they are fear, but not the fear of Allah. The first is a feeling of which anyone should be ashamed.

[3] By doing all that He has ordered and by abstaining from all that He has forbidden.

# Foundations
# of Islamic Civilisation

Rites And Rituals: The foundation of Islamic civilisation lies in building character, and the attitude towards life and death, and the worlds here and hereafter. To attain this goal the rites of *iman – salat, sawm, hajj and zakat* – are compulsory upon all. These rites are to be followed and practised in such a way that the principles involved are reflected in the deeds and behaviours of each Muslim. For example, iman in Allah is affirmed in the way that the muminun are absolutely dependent on Allah's help and will in leading their lives, filled as they are, with pain and pleasure.

Similarly, the *salat* trains the mumin both in psyche and manners to play his small part in upholding honesty, both in word and deed, at the cost even of life. To worship Allah, *salat* is first the compulsory prayer, performed by Muslims five times a day taking only ten to fifteen minutes each time. It has now been shown by some studies that *salat* is also the best exercise for the human body. Surveys have found that the true Muslim who performs *salat* regularly lives longer than the average man.

*Sawm* means fasting in the month of Ramadan, i.e. not to have food, drink or sexual relations from before *fajr* (early morning prayers) until sunset. Fasting makes him capable of resisting immorality and poverty without surrendering to temptations.

Likewise *hajj*, (the pilgrimage to Makkah) teaches him that he is a global being in instituting and enforcing the qualities that he attains through the above rites and commitments.

Lastly *zakat* prepares him to earn wealth, both for himself and for the downtrodden in such a way that he becomes the master of money, not its slave, in earning and spending. *Zakat* is the fixed proportion (two and a half per cent on cash, i.e. gold and silver, and certain proportions of cattle, and either ten or twenty percent of crops such as pulses and grains, etc.) of a Muslim's wealth and property that is liable to be paid for the benefit of the poor in the community, the indebted, for the release of slaves, for work done in the way of Allah, etc. The payment of *zakat* is obligatory as it is one of the five pillars of Islam. A by-product of *zakat* is that it is a major economic means for establishing social justice and leading the poorer sections of human society to prosperity and security.

Now all these rites are, it is evident, committed to the welfare of both the individual and the community. Any deviation from these noble attitudes and practices, is cruel exploitation and hence is non-, un- and anti- Islamic. If such inhuman propensities were allowed to continue unchecked, they would mean the annihilation of human society, or the absolute extinction of human life by degrees. The Creator of the universe is ultimately never seen to allow such forces to go unpunished, whether in this world or in the unseen. The stories of Haman, Nimrod, Fir'awn (Pharaoh), etc., are glaring examples from which we and posterity can learn this lesson.

Here it should be noted, with special attention, that *jihad* is another injunction incumbent on all muslims. *Jihad* is struggling and fighting in the way of Allah, or any other kind of effort to make Allah's word the uppermost and fight against evil. The Prophet (SAAS) said the greatest *jihad* is to fight with oneself, to save yourself from evil. Both good and evil deeds are done with power and strength. It is essential that the good deeds should be the superior in power, to restore the activities essential to human welfare, in the face of wrong forces and intrigues. Allah is the All-Powerful, and His slaves should have such qualities and traits of character as to make manifest the traditional saying, "Adorn yourselves with the qualities of Allah", to prove yourself the slaves of a Creator Who is All-Powerful, and Who alone is Almighty.

The Prophet Muhammad's (SAAS) life and character was unparalleled because he was endangered by the fights and battles that followed him until his death. Islam would not have endured if there were not the battles of Badr, Uhud and Khandaq, some of the first battles fought by the Muslims. The ever-shining glory of the Islamic community of the Prophet Muhammad (SAAS) AND his Khulafa ar-Rashidun (the four greatest companions of Muhammad (SAAS) and the first four Caliphs) rests absolutely on their sparkling swords that were committed to fighting for the sake of Allah, and to attain the welfare of the people and land. Their prayers and other rites had always been nurtured, nourished and made to flourish by their martial arts and valour. Hence to some Muslims *jihad* should almost be considered an additional pillar of Islam.

The manner is the man. The difference between him and other creatures is due to his 'manner'. It makes his intellect and heart supreme over his animality, which always tends to debase him and undo morality and justice. This refinement is attained through the conscientious practice of the rites above.

In addition, there are also specifications of manner and behaviour. For instance, a true Muslim is defined in a *hadith* (a tradition accurately recorded from the Prophet (SAAS)) as a person from whose words and deeds other Muslims are safe. It means that when he speaks or talks to others or about them in their absence, he is not abusive, nor indecent, both in the words spoken and in his heart. He is gentle and polite throughout.

Again, when taking food and drink, he restrains greed and avoids overeating. This is because Islam teaches that excess food and drink not only cause harm to health and body, but also invites economic disaster in the form of extravagance leading to poverty. *Sawm*, or fasting, as viewed by the doctors of modern times, is considered a protection against diabetics, high blood-pressure and allied ills. Thus we see in the rites of Islam good health-rules for those who follow them heartily.

Similarly *salat,* in congregation or under the leadership of Islam, makes the muminun accustomed to leading disciplined and honest lives under a single and unified command. Again, if it is seen that the command goes against the injunctions of the Noble Qur'an and the Sunnah (the customary practice of the Prophet (SAAS) and of his Khulafa ar-Rashidun that is the model the Muslims follow), the followers have the full right and authority to disobey the commander. If his command amounts to kufr, they must replace him by a suitable one in order to maintain peace and justice in the society. That means *salat* is not merely a prayer, rather it is a training process for attaining a united community of Muslims irrespective of the man-made norms of politics such as land, language, colour or blood. Rather Islam stresses a great deal *taqwa,* or the Allah-fearing character, of the man to be the head of the community. His qualities of statesmanship, rather than his ability to manipulate people for politics, consist in the traits of honesty, sincerity, efficiency, justice, the qualities that promote a man to attain, in mounting degrees, the proximity of Allah's love and bliss. It goes without saying that he must be skilled in leading people in peace and in war.

In the Noble Qur'an Allah says:

"If My slaves ask you about Me, I am near. I answer the call of the caller when he calls on Me. They should therefore respond to Me and believe in Me so that hopefully they will be rightly guided." (Surat al-Baqarah: 186)

"Allah has promised those of you who have iman and do right actions that He will make them successors in the land as He made those before them successors, and will firmly establish for them their deen with which He is pleased and give them, in place of their fear, security. 'They worship Me, not associating anything with Me.' Any who are kafir after that, such people are deviators." (Surat an-Nur 24: 55)

Now let us see what are the views of doctors and physicians of modern times on the rites of Islam, viewed from the standpoint of medical science.

The celebrated physician Doctor Graham, for instance, opines that *sawm* in

Islam is seen to alleviate the pains of peptic ulcer and reduce the burning intensity of it remarkably. Doctor Isaac Jening, on the other hand, remarks on the laziness of the food practices of modern people, and that these habits have, by little steps, dragged such people towards self-destructive consequences. Doctor M.A. Rahat also echoes the same warning. According to him the habit of excessive food-intake causes problems in the stomach. To get rid of all these troubles and diseases, *sawm* or fasting plays an excellent role in the human body.

To Doctor Joyalce, fasting helps the human body enjoy disease-free periods during starvation. Doctor Alex Heig is of the opinion that fasting sharpens the power of memory, enhances the capacity for reasoning and devotion to works and contemplation. Doctor Dewan, one of the celebrated physicians of South-East Asia, expresses almost the identical view, when he says the observation of fasting rejuvenates the brain and the nerves of human beings. Similarly the world-famed Doctor Stanley Davidson has found that *sawm* helps maintain the balance of cholesterol, and prevents excessive fat from being stored in the stomach. As a result someone who fasts rids his body of diabetes and hypertension, easily and comfortably.

The science of nutrition has recently made it apparent that Islam's directives regarding the prohibitions and prescriptions relating to taking *haram* (unlawful, forbidden and punishable from the viewpoint of Islam) and *halal* (lawful from the viewpoint of Islam) foods and drinks, are perfectly and absolutely in conformity with good practice, where concerned with health and a strong mind. For example, beef, mutton and chicken are made *halal* by the Qur'an because of the fact that the flesh of these animals does not contain elements that are detrimental to the human body, blood and fibre. As these are mild in temperament and are neither dirty nor poisonous, Allah has made the meat of these gentle animals *halal*. Their meat if taken helps us grow and nourishes gentility, cleanliness and wholesome feelings in the human body and soul. Conversely animals like boars, pigs, tigers, and snakes etc., are, by nature, wild and aggressive, and also poisonous, and hence the flesh of such animals is strictly forbidden for mankind. Likewise alcoholic drinks, that excite people and arouse their sexual appetites for short periods, and make people shameless in their nature and dealings are also *haram*, i.e. forbidden (as are earnings from the sale of these items), although they have some merits which are very small in comparison to their faults. Medical science has made experiments on the effects of alcoholic drinks and come to the conclusion that such drinks are detrimental.

They:

1. Spoil the digestive system
2. Deform the beauty of the human face and harm our health
3. Weaken the nerves and respiratory system and spoil kidneys and liver
4. Prematurely deform the body and intellect with age
5. Harm sexual capacity and
6. Cause moral turpitude.

Not only these. Forbidden food and drinks are the cause of horrific matters such as insanity, murder, sexual-harassment, reckless driving which in turn causes fatal accidents, and the threat, nowadays, of the almost total annihilation of the moral virtues underlying all human culture and civilisation. Seeing the horrible consequences of alcohol in modern society a German doctor expressed the conviction that: "If half of the warehouses of wine and alcohol were closed down, there would be no need for half of the hospitals and prisons of the world."

For maintaining good health, Allah (SWT) has laid down sound health rules that are, indeed, divine directives for modern health and sanitation. For instance, He has made it incumbent upon each individual to earn his bread by honest sweat and toil. It means he has been confined to businesses that are *halal* and to spending his wealth in ways that are also *halal* in nature and operation. As a result he cannot employ his mind, money and energy in *haram* businesses like usury, trading in alcohol, etc. Following such restrictions on economic activities, a man becoming well-to-do has to spend his surplus for the benefit of the poor of his society in the form of creating opportunities, and also by giving *zakat, sadaqah* (anything given in charity) to the people still without income from the lack of opportunities. Overspending and extravagance are *haram* and, therefore, a rich muslim has neither the mind nor the opportunity for hedonistic culture.

To develop such attitudes and behaviour and to help himself to attain humanitarian and moral qualities, a man has, according to the teachings of Islam, to discipline his tastes and likings by the practices of, for example, taking food with his right hand, speaking to others in mild unhurtful words, sleeping without snoring to avoid disturbing the sleep of friends, etc. And to make himself noble and almost angelic in mind and manner, the first word of the Qur'an revealed is *iqra* – recite/read, so that mankind can enlighten themselves in this manner. This is the only way for him to be the viceroy of Allah on earth.

Allah is the only divine Being. None other than He may be worshipped. Then the Prophet Muhammad (SAAS) is to be followed as well as possible, in order to properly abide by His directives. Third, parents are to be obeyed unless this obedience contradicts Allah's injunctions – provided a man wants to live a useful life of *taqwa* in this mortal world. It is clear from *hadith* that in the satisfaction of muslim parents lies one of the means to the satisfaction of Allah. Children are warned that the Garden lay at the feet of their mothers. In another *hadith* there is mention that the door of the children's Garden is their father; so on and so forth.

Thus it is evident that if such values of Islam were now imbued in the thought and behaviour of the young, the present world, now engulfed with so many ills and misfortunes, would certainly have that real salvation upon which the peaceful life of Adam's descendants is absolutely dependant.

Of all the harrowing problems of the modern age, sexuality is presently becoming one of the crucial ones for mankind. It is certainly one of the core problems for our spiritual life and existence. Sexuality is common to all creatures and it is a gift of nature bestowed upon them to maintain their species, while facing the annihilation of decay and death from the very inception of life on earth. Man, being the best of creation, is commanded to exercise his sexuality in matrimony, under terms and conditions laid down by his Creator. He is, therefore, under compulsion to abide by all these rules for attaining sublimity in his sexual life and dealings. And abiding by these conditions is one of the factors that has made man a noble creation on earth.

Sexuality is for animals exclusively a matter of enjoyment, but for man, it is both a joy and an obligation in order to institute a flourishing society bathed in decency. He is basically a moral being and hence his 'animality' is to be formed and influenced by it until his last breath. Otherwise, his society would be akin to the society of beasts and wild animals or indeed worse because when man does not fulfil his human destiny he is much worse than the animals.

The tales of the Noble Qur'an have picturesque descriptions of a great many peoples whose defiance of the moralities of sex led to horrific ruin. These description are of universal significance for our guidance and the generations to come.

Minute study of the rise and fall of past civilisations shows that the rise was constant when they, both males and females, had morality-based sexual relations, but they were to witness an all-downward trend after defying the code of ethics and morality in enjoying sex. It is axiomatic that the ruination of a man, his society and country occurs when the three "Ws" – wine, women and war dictate to them. One of the roots of such a disaster is an immoral sexual-culture.

The question is raised by some, in our so-called 'modern' society, as to why Islam permits polygamy. Here, in this context, let us see what Dr. Annie Besant, President of the Theosophical Society, has said in her book Beauties of Islam. She writes:

> "The true and righteous sex-relation between one man and one woman is preached as an ideal in some countries, but is generally practised in none. Islam permits polygamy; Christendom forbids but winks at it,

provided that no legal tie exists with more than one. There is pretended monogamy in the West, but there is really polygamy without responsibility; the 'mistress' is cast off when the man is weary of her, and sinks, gradually to be the woman of the streets, for the first lover has no responsibility for her future, and she is a hundred times worse off than the sheltered wife and mother in the polygamous home. When we see the thousands of miserable women who crowd the streets of Western towns during the night, we must surely feel that it does not lie in Western mouths to reproach Islam for its polygamy."

In the same work the author then eulogises the principles of Islam in safeguarding the weaker sex in the following way:

"It is better for a woman, happier for a woman, more respectable for a woman, to live in Mohammedan polygamy, united to one man only with legitimate children in her arms, and surrounded with respect than to be seduced, cast out into the streets – perhaps with an illegitimate child outside the pale of law, unsheltered and uncared for, to become a victim of any passer-by, night after night, rendered incapable of motherhood, despised by all."

Two essays published by Islamic Council of Europe in 1976, by two European Muslim ladies, one by Mrs. Ayesha Lemu and the other by Fatima Heeren, also deserve minute attention, when studying the fate of womenfolk under monogamy and polygamy. Mrs. Ayesha Lemu, for instance, writes:

"One should, therefore, regard monogamy as the norm, and polygamy as the exception... polygamy has under certain circumstances a valuable function. In some situations it may be considered as the lesser of two evils; in others as a positively beneficial arrangement. The most obvious example of this occurs in times of war when there are inevitably large members of widows and girls whose fiances and husbands have been killed in fighting... If it is still maintained that under these circumstances a man marry only one wife, what options are left to the millions of other women who have no hope of getting a husband? Their choice, bluntly stated, is between a chaste and childless old maidenhood or to become somebody's mistress – that is, an unofficial second wife with no legal rights for herself, or for her children. Most women would not welcome either of these, since most women have always wanted and still do want the security of a legal husband and family. For women under these circumstances compromise may be their only choice. Given the alternative, many of them would rather share a husband than have none at all."

Fatima Heeren's opinion also deserves the same appreciation when she is seen to agree:

"Before the Registrar married me to my European Muslim husband, he warned me of the four wives which would be admissible to him if we should ever live in a Muslim country. Though a bit awestruck at first, I soon learned that just because having more than one wife is allowed in Islam, it is practised very seldom. And since this official concession to the polygamous disposition (which is) undoubtedly inherent in some men, or to extraordinary circumstances, like constant illness or barrenness of the first wife, on the other hand completely prohibits sexual relations outside marriage, I hold it to be a very wise decision. If a Muslim man for this or that reason simply cannot help desiring more than one wife, he is not forced by this urge to resort to any sinful act but may quite lawfully enjoy its fulfilment along with shouldering the consequent responsibilities."

The French advocate, Dr. Le Bon, holds the opinion that polygamy is the only way to save the society from sexual-evils. In his words:

"A return to polygamy, the natural relation between the sexes would remedy many evils: prostitution, venereal diseases, abortion, the misery of illegitimate children, the misfortune of millions of unmarried women, resulting from disproportion between the sexes, adultery and even jealousy, since the disregarded wife would find consolation in her cognizance of not being secretly deceived by her husband".

Dr. Le Bon forecasts, with almost unshakable conviction, that "European legislation will recognize polygamy as an institution in the future" for the salvation of Europe an abyss of horrible sex-crimes especially in English society and the nation as a whole. In his celebrated work *Muhammad, The Final Messenger*, Advocate Le Bon tried to make readers aware that, unless polygamy is fairly and honestly admitted into society, Europe, as the leading continent of human civilisation and culture on the globe, will lose its glory and power to the extent of almost complete extinction.

In his discourse *Conduct and Disorders Biologically Considered*, Dr. Mercier draws the conclusion that "Woman is by nature a monogamist; man has in him the elements of a polygamist." The famed philosopher Schopenhauer asserts: "There is no use arguing about polygamy; it must be taken as *de facto* existing everywhere, and the only question is to how it shall be regulated."

According to Max Nordau, "Man lives in a state of polygamy in the civilised countries in spite of monogamy enforced by law; out of a hundred thousand men there would have barely been one who could swear upon his deathbed that he had never known but one single woman during his whole life." Mr. Max Nordau, a prominent philosophical writer, studied the marital conditions of the countries and societies where polygamy is not recognised by religion or morality, and the above quotation, taken from his book *Conventional Lies of Our Civilization,* reflects on the character of those countries and societies. Polygamy is not a bad show, rather it is a positive contribution to society, uplifting and maintaining the moral virtues and beauties upon which the mental and material peace and development of human society fundamentally depends.

Dr. MacFarlane has attributed these qualities to polygamy. In his essay, *The case for polygamy,* MacFarlane remarks, "Whether the question is considered socially or religiously, it can be demonstrated that polygamy is not contrary to the highest standards of civilisation. The suggestion offers a practical remedy for the Western problem of the destitute and unwanted female, the alternative is continued and increased prostitution, concubinage and distressing spinsterhood".

The above quotations from different authors have made it clear why polygamy is a blessing to mankind, and that the false pretence to monogamy, with its concomitant covert adultery, has been eating up the vitality of Western character and civilisation.

Now we shall turn to Islam and see why Allah has approved polygamy side by side with monogamy and has sanctioned polygamy under certain conditions.

In the Noble Qur'an Allah says:

**"If you are afraid of not behaving justly towards orphans, then marry other permissible women, two, three or four. But if you are afraid of not treating them equally, then only one, or those you own as slaves. That makes it more likely that you will not be unfair."** (Surah 4: 3)

Physical fitness, economic capability and the determination to be fair to all the wives are the conditions for a Muslim man entering into more than one marriage. If such conditions are not adhered to, and not practised in reality, it would be a wrong action for him to have more than one wife. Our Prophet (SAAS) warned the man who has two wives that, on the Day of Judgement, half of his body would be buried in the ground, if he fails to be fair to his wives according to the injunctions of the Noble Qur'an. And such an appalling situation would linger until he was thrown into the Fire, unless Allah forgave.

Mu'adh ibn Jabal (RA), for instance, a companion of the Prophet Muhammad (SAAS), had two wives who died of plague at the same time, and Jabal had difficulty in respect of taking the decision to entomb them with equal honour and status. That means a true Muslim, having more than one wife, should have to have a great deal of care and alertness in maintaining his conjugal life with his wives. As a result, it is clear that to have four wives at a time, abiding by the conditions imposed by Islam, is a tremendous responsibility. The Prophet Muhammad (SAAS) had more than one wife after the death of his first wife Khadijah (RA), during whose lifetime he did not feel the need of any other woman's company. Rather he later used to praise her as a lady accomplished in mind and manner before his other wives and asked them not to compare her with any one of them, as that might offend him.

History speaks of his sublime and magnanimous soul with reference to his other marriages. To award shelter, honour and security of life to them, he married the other ladies, who had rank and status in their parental heritage or from earlier weddings. All his (SAAS) wives, excepting A'ishah (RA), were widows or divorced women. It means that in Islam multiple marriages are advocated mainly on humanitarian grounds.

To check and uproot sexual crime and immodesty from society, it is not unusual for Muslim parents to give their daughters in marriage soon after they reach puberty. It does not mean that Islam favours child marriage. Rather, it is advisable for parents to arrange the wedding having the mutual consent of the proposed bride and bridegroom, so that their wedding tie does not break up from mere whims or emotions. Second, a poverty-stricken youth is advised not to marry until he becomes capable economically of maintaining his conjugal life in a decent manner. He is advised to practise restraining his sexual urges, by fasting if necessary, while he gains economic solvency.

Now it is clear that 'Islam' is the only way with at least the potential to protect people against immoral sex and its unbridled exploitation.

The veil-system in Islam is another divine step imposed to control and regulate healthy and honourable relation between the sexes. In the Noble Qur'an Allah says:

**"O Prophet! Tell your wives and daughters and the women of the muminun to draw their outer garments closely round themselves. This**

makes it more likely that they will be recognised and not be harmed. Allah is Ever-Forgiving, Most Merciful." (Surah 33: 59)

Allah has made man and woman in such a manner that each one is attractive to the other, and especially the structure and shape of woman is very appealing to man's passions and senses. That is why it is said that one Helen is sufficiently powerful to destroy Troy, or one Cleopatra to demolish Egypt. This is to say that the weaker sex is more able than other males to bring total disaster upon a man, just as the stone, though hard, is melted by fire though fire is apparently weak in appearance.

Allah has made man powerful than woman in many ways. Medical science shows there is a difference between men's and women's brain in weight as well as in size and composition. The weight of the average man's brain is between a maximum of 65 ounces and a minimum of 38 ounces. The average woman's brain it is between 45 and 31 ounces respectively. In addition psychologists have also measured that a woman's brain has lesser waves than these of men. Two prominent doctors, viz. Nicholas and Baley, have shown that conclusively. Nevertheless, the size and weight of the brain, as we know, prove nothing, since if it were by weight alone, the elephant must be the most intelligent of all creatures. However, what this result shows, is what we know anyway, which is that man is not like woman.

The five senses of women are different to those of man. Smell, perception, physical strength, thickness of muscles and flesh, body-weight, psychology and heartbeat, etc., are not identical in the sexes. This distinction is made by Allah and so it is a universal phenomena about which no one can do anything, unless he or she is committed to bringing disaster upon the human species. That is why in some respects man has an edge over woman, for which the Noble Qur'an declares that, "…**men have a degree above them.**" (Surat al-Baqarah: 226) and, "**Men have charge of women because Allah has preferred the one above the other and because they spend their wealth on them.**" (Surah an-Nisa: 34) So man is the protector of woman in all respects. At the same time the Noble Qur'an warns him not to be self-centred in handling her private and social affairs. The noble Qur'an declares, **"They are clothing for you and you for them."** (Surat al-Baqarah: 186) In the noble Qur'an Allah says:

> **"Women possess rights similar to those held over them to be honoured with fairness; but men have a degree above them."** (Surah 2: 228)

So it is now transparent that it is only in Islam that man and woman, though physiologically and psychologically different in many aspects and respects, are said to be coequal in enjoying socio-religio-economic, and even political lives. The importance of the mother and motherhood is made so significant that it is said that the Garden of children lies under the feet of the mother. Again elsewhere we are warned that no husband shall enter the Garden unless he is certified good in character by his wife.

Before the advent of Muhammad (SAAS) as the last Prophet, the conditions of womenfolk were miserable in the extreme. Ancient Roman senators, for instance, considered womenfolk as dirty beasts possessing no soul; mediaeval Christendom treated them as the gateway of the devil and, therefore, for their bringing evils into society they had no value as human beings; the Arabs of old times viewed having a female child in a family as a weakness since it exposed the family to the humiliation of having the girl abducted and hence infanticide of girl children was sometimes practised in their barbaric community. Ancient India offers us a similar gloomy picture. The *satidaha,* or so-called religious system of making a wife jump onto the pyre of dead husband for salvation, was so harrowing that the remembrance of it still causes shuddering in our bodies and blood.

Now modern Europe has introduced the same barbaric rules in the guise of art and culture. Free-mixing, dating, and cohabitation with mutual consent are now in vogue in most European countries, not excepting the UK. The same wind has almost blown in the countries of other continents of the globe. And it seems that sexuality has become the pivot of human art, culture, music and commerce, through which fatal venereal diseases, plus the most horrific one, AIDS, threaten millions of hedonists and epicureans enjoying their lives and luxuries.

Sexual violation, sexual harassment, sexual crime now appear to rule quite recklessly almost every level of society in such a way that governments face a tremendously dangerous situation in containing these forces. Many of the major leaders, heads of states, celebrated poets and leaders of civilised countries are themselves rarely seen as innocent of such crimes and wrong actions, but yet they are regarded as the guardians of modern civilisation! That means that now illicit sex, unless brought to court, is no longer considered a wrong.

Hence instead of cultivating deen and morality in enjoying sex, modern people are trying to invent an antidote for AIDS, so that sexual enjoyment is not handicapped by the fatal consequences which are now of great concern to immorally sexually-oriented peoples. Man has gone far in transgressing the Divine command!

### The Position of Women in Islam
Some of the enemies of Islam, or those with a lack of knowledge of it, say that Islam disregards women and that they are kept at home, behind doors. We would like to ask them: do they really hold women in regard? The answer is no. They are using women – in the streets, on advertising posters, in the cinemas, with many having to take their clothes off, and in many other ways that it is not necessary to discuss here.

They are treating women virtually as animals that they can use as they please. They have taken flowers from the garden and thrown them in the streets. They have taken life-partners as bed-partners only, to be entertained by them as they desire. Their women are now their dancing dolls. They use them whenever and wherever they desire. The enjoyment of a women's companionship is now a thing made easy for them. That which is easy to find and easy to acquire has no value. Today their women have no special value, and the day is not far off when they will have no value at all.

Now we can look again at that verse of the noble Qur'an, where Allah says:

**"O Prophet! Tell your wives and daughters and the women of the muminun to draw their outer garments closely round themselves. This makes it more likely that they will be recognised and not be harmed. Allah is Ever-Forgiving, Most Merciful." (Surah 33: 59)**

Naturally women are designed to have the responsibility of family and house, and men to work and earn and to give women full financial and physical protection, with kind and respectful treatment. But Islam did not ask women only to stay at home. They can go out, be educated (which is mandated for both men and women in Islam), take part in the events of society, run businesses, and do jobs if it is necessary for them to do so, but while "draw their outer garments closely round themselves", as the Qur'an says. Then they will be safe, and it will increase their distinctive values in which they excel men. Women should not become as open as men, they should not be as easy as men, they should not be as easily available as men. This will protect their attractiveness and maintain their values at the highest. This is the nature of women. If you go against nature you will be in danger. That is the reason for suffering in the present-day world. Women are not safe today, except for a few, true Muslim women.

Islam has given women opportunities equal to men – in some ways even more. But it has asked them only: save the greater value of your distinction, because you are the most beautiful creation of the Lord, the Creator Allah. So save yourselves and be honoured and respected. Then you will see that you will be loved honestly more than anything in the world.

Here are some of the rights of women, in the light of the Qur'an, and the Prophet Muhammad's (SAAS) *Sunnah*:

1. Human rights. Islam established women's equality with man in her humanity over 1,400 years ago. In the Noble Qur'an Allah says:

**"O mankind! have taqwa of your Lord who created you from a single**

self and created its mate from it and then disseminated many men and women from the two of them. Have taqwa of Allah in whose name you make demands on one another and also in respect of your families. Allah watches over you continually." (Surat an-Nisa: 1)

2. Civil rights. In Islam women are encouraged to contribute their thoughts and views. There are many *hadith* of the Prophet Muhammad (SAAS) which indicate that women would pose questions directly to him, and offer their views and advice concerning the deen, economics and social matters. A Muslim woman chooses whether or not to accept the proposal of her husband, or she herself proposes marriage, and keeps her name after marriage. A Muslim woman's testimony is valid in legal disputes.

3. Social rights. The Prophet Muhammad (SAAS) said: "Seeking knowledge is obligatory for every Muslim, male and female." Man and woman both have the capacity for learning and understanding. Also it is their obligation to promote good behaviour and condemn bad behaviour in all spheres of life, and Muslim women must acquire the appropriate education to perform such duties, in accordance with their own natural talents and interests.

While maintaining her home and providing support for her husband, the raising and teaching of children are among the most highly regarded roles for a Muslim woman. If she has the skills to work outside her home, in a way which is good for her and for the community, she may certainly do so, as long as her family obligations are met.

Islam recognises and fosters the natural difference between men and women, despite their equality. Some types of work are more suitable for men, some more suitable for women. This in no way diminishes either's efforts or its benefits. Allah will reward both of them for the value of their work, though it may not necessarily have been the same sort of work, or type of activity.

Concerning motherhood the Prophet Muhammad (SAAS) said words to the effect that: "The Garden lies at the feet of the mother". This implies that the success of a society or a nation is to be traced to the mothers that raised it. So, therefore, a woman must be educated and conscientious in order to be a skilled parent, for the sake of the family, society and nation.

4. Political rights. A Muslim woman must pledge allegiance to the ruler as do the men. A Muslim woman may express her knowledge on any public matter, and participate in the political arena. According to Islamic history, Muslim women occasionally even took part in the fighting during battles. Islam does not even forbid a woman from holding important government positions. Abd ar-Rahman ibn 'Auf (one of Muhammad's (SAAS) companions) consulted many men and women before he recommended that 'Uthman ibn 'Affan (RA) be the Caliph.

5. Economic rights. In the noble Qur'an Allah says:

**"Do not covet what Allah has given to some of you in preference to others – men have a portion of what they acquire and women have a portion of what they acquire; but ask Allah for His bounty. Allah has knowledge of all things." (Surah 4: 32)**

A Muslim woman has the right to earn money, do her own business, own property, enter into legal contracts, and manage all of her assets in any way she pleases. No one can claim any share of her business, property or her earnings, including her husband, unless she wishes it. Although her husband has the full responsibility to maintain her with financial support. In the noble Qur'an Allah says: **"Men have charge of women because Allah has preferred the one above the other and because they spend their wealth on them." (Surah 4: 34)**

Although man has the duty to protect woman and maintain her from his wealth, he has no right to claim anything from her property, business or earnings. She can manage them, use them or spend them as she pleases.

So the conclusion is that Islam has given women, not only equality, but even more opportunities, more respect and regard than men. No other religion has given half as much.

Let us briefly see what Judaeo-Christians say about women. The Catholic Bible states explicitly that, "The birth of a daughter is a loss." (Ecclesiasticus 22: 3). But, in contrast to this shocking statement, boys receive special praise: "A man who educates his son will be the envy of his enemy." (Ecclesiasticus 30:3).

A daughter is always considered a painful burden, a potential source of shame to her father: "Your daughter is headstrong? Keep a sharp lookout that she does not make you the laughing-stock of your enemies, the talk of the town, the object of common gossip, and put you to public shame." (Ecclesiasticus 42: 11). "Keep a headstrong daughter under firm control or she will abuse any indulgence she receives. Keep strict watch on her shameless eye, do not be surprised if she disgraces you." (Ecclesiasticus 26: 10-11)

The above conceptions regarding women are limited to the newly-born or young, but Judaeo-Christian views extend far beyond that. Let us compare their attitudes to a woman trying to learn her own religion. The heart of Judaism is the Torah, "the Law". However according to the Talmud, "Women are exempt from the study of the Torah."

The attitude of St. Paul in the New Testament is: "As in all the congregations of the saints, women should remain silent in the churches. They are not allowed to speak, but must be in submission as the Law says. If they want to inquire about something, they should ask their own husbands at home, for it is disgraceful for a woman to speak in the church." (1 Corinthians 14: 34-35)

Now the crucial question is: how will a woman learn if she is not allowed to speak? How can a woman grow intellectually if she is obliged to be in a state of full submission? How can she broaden her horizons if her one and only source of information is her husband at home? Here Islam says that education and the acquisition of knowledge is equally mandatory for both men and women.

In contrast to the Bible, the Qur'an considers that the birth of a female is a gift and a blessing from Allah, the same as the birth of a male. The Qur'an even mentions the gift of a female birth first. In the Qur'an Allah says:

**"The kingdom of the heavens and earth belongs to Allah. He creates whatever He wills. He gives daughters to whoever He wishes; and He gives sons to whoever He wishes; or He gives them both sons and daughters; and He makes whoever He wishes barren. Truly He is All-Knowing, All-Powerful." (Surat ash-Shura: 46)**

In *hadith* the Prophet Muhammad (SAAS) said, "He who is involved in bringing up daughters, and accords benevolent treatment towards them, they will be protection for him against the Fire." (Al-Bukhari and Muslim).

**Sayings of the Prophet (SAAS) about Women:**
❍     Women are the twin half of man.

❍     Allah commands you to treat women well, for they are your mothers, daughters and aunts.

❍     The rights of women are sacred. See, therefore, that women are maintained in the rights granted to them.

❍     And the best of you are those who are kindest to their wives.

# The Oneness of the Creator and of His Deen

In the light of science, not to embrace Islam is foolishness, because Islam and science are as alike as twin sisters. Islam is the only deen which is fully consistent with human nature. It is a complete code of life, and to every aspect of man Islam guarantees peace, prosperity and happiness. This has been proved during the last fourteen hundred years. A true Muslim (a real follower of Islam) is the best man in human society. And the best man is guaranteed to lead his life with peace, happiness and joy, and with endless peace, happiness and joy in the life hereafter.

There is only one Creator or God, so He must have only one deen. Islam is the only natural deen for mankind, the best and most complete code of life. This life must be lived with peace, prosperity and happiness. This is a scientific view, and proved in reality. Otherwise man's life is afflicted with sadness, sorrow and difficulties. Without peace, without a purpose or destination in his busy life – suddenly man dies one day.

The one deen of Allah is Islam, which is embodied in human nature. So man should follow his natural way of life – Islam – for his own sake, to enjoy the best life, here and hereafter.

Here are some verses from the noble Qur'an, as Allah, the All-Mighty God says:

**"Allah has no son and there is no other god accompanying Him, for then each god would have gone off with what he created and one of them would have been exalted above the other. Glory be to Allah above what they describe, Knower of the Unseen and the Visible! May He be exalted above all they associate with Him!" (Surah 23: 91)**

"Today I have perfected your deen for you and completed My blessing upon you and I am pleased with Islam as a deen for you." (Surah 5: 3)

"He has laid down the same deen for you as He enjoined on Nuh: that which We have revealed to you and which We enjoined on Ibrahim, Musa and 'Isa: 'Establish the deen and do not make divisions in it.'" (Surah 42: 13)

"Yes, the friends of Allah will feel no fear and will know no sorrow: those who have iman and show taqwa, there is good news for them in the life of the dunya[1] and in the akhira[2]. There is no changing the words of Allah. That is the great victory!" (Surah 10: 62-64)

Islam says every human is born in the natural condition, whether the child's parents were Muslims or not. The child is naturally born with a pure nature, and Islam is the deen of the natural condition. So all the acts and activities of Islam are embodied within human nature, for people's own best interests. But when the child grows, and if he moves away from his own nature (which is Islam), particularly because of the efforts of his parents and his society, then he becomes non-Muslim. But he will still have the chance to embrace Islam at any time, and own all the beauties and goodness of his own nature which is Islam.

Islam is always modern and, even now, Islam is far more progressive than our modern times. Much of what science has produced in the past, what science is producing in the present and what science will produce in the future, the noble Qur'an, or Islam, has already foreseen over fourteen hundred years ago. Further developments in science, day by day, will make understanding the noble Qur'an easier.

Islam makes man well-civilised, and shows the way to lead modern life. Islam guarantees happiness and a peaceful and healthy life. This is not a tale but has been proved for the last fourteen hundred years. Please read history.

---

[1, 2] See the Glossary on page 88

There is no problem of man for which Islam or the noble Qur'an cannot be used to find a solution. What more can we ask for? We have everything, as we are the supreme creation of the Creator of the universe. Supreme creatures' lives should reflect that supremacy, and not be filled with sadness and sorrow over problems and difficulties. Man deserves to live in peace and happiness, but that will only happen if he lives in accordance with his own nature, Islam.

**Guarantees of Islam**

Islam offers man the guarantee of a life free from infestation with problems. There is not a single problem the solution for which has not been given by the noble Qur'an or the prophetic Sunnah.

Allah says:

> "'You will soon know who will receive a punishment which disgraces him and will unleash against himself an everlasting punishment.' We have sent down to you the Book for mankind with truth. So whoever is guided is guided to his own good and whoever is misguided, it is to his detriment. You are not set over them as a guardian." (Surah 39: 37-38)

The ayat above have made it transparent that the Qur'an is for the welfare of man provided he is earnest and sincere in following it, and that also he alone will have to sustain the consequences of going astray. Allah says:

> "No indeed! It is truly a reminder to which anyone who wills may pay heed." (Surah 74: 54-55)

Hence it is an axiomatic truth that for guidance and prosperity, the noble Qur'an along with the Sunnah are the absolute and fully adequate authorities for mankind to win peace and prosperity in this world and the world hereafter.

However the term 'peace' is absolutely abstract in its essence and nature.

And so the people who think of peace only in terms of wealth and riches, power and human resources, naturally fall prey to anxiety and worry about the loss of all their material wealth, in any form or description.

As a result, we are used to coming across the tragic ends of many so-called rich people, dying of heart attacks, by accident, killings or poisonings, etc., because of false friends or foes, or committing suicide to get rid of the pangs and pricks of losing their riches, etc. Indeed, it is seen that wife and children, money and property, always tend to throw the so-called rich man into anxiety.

In the Noble Qur'an Allah remarks:

> **"Do not let their wealth and children impress you. Allah merely wants to punish them by them during their life in the dunya and for them to expire while they are kuffar." (Surah 9: 55)**

Worshippers of wealth, money and power think that such property and belongings make them permanent on the earth, in body, mind and riches. But alas! ultimately they find themselves engulfed in mental torture and agonies that hasten their woeful deaths on this mortal earth. They go mad and are seen to be panting like greedy dogs. Their tragic condition has already been depicted in the following way:

> **"His metaphor is that of a dog: if you chase it away, it lolls out its tongue and pants, and if you leave it alone, it lolls out its tongue and pants. That is the metaphor of those who deny Our Signs." (Surah 7: 176)**

Allah, the Almighty feeds them and allows them to lead such a life with a view to making them reach their maturity in their misdeeds, so that they get proper and absolute punishment in the worlds here and hereafter. Such people never achieve mental peace in their mature lives, and beauty and pleasure are fragile. When they feel that their heart is in the Fire, they become addicted to opium, wine, liquor, etc., and sometimes slide into immoral and sensuous pleasure and debaucheries. Now it is quite apparent that a simple life is better by far, and more wholesome, than a life full of such riches and pleasures from which mental peace and morals are driven out.

But being rich and wealthy is not a bad thing for a true Muslim. He can give zakat and extra voluntary sadaqah which is good for society, and also he can perform hajj (pilgrimage) which is one of the five pillars of Islam for those who are able to do it. But for a muslim to be rich is not for him to be addicted to money and wealth, which will make him forget his Creator, Allah, and his own nature, and lead a life in a way that will leave him anxious, sad and full of sorrows, with problems, a troubled life and endless punishment, here and in the hereafter. To be rich, as a true Muslim, you do not have to work very hard, or be very busy, because there is always mercy and help from Allah for you.

The following story – a true story – is appropriate to illustrate the above situation for us.

I know a true Muslim who has a small clothes shop. At the time of salat (prayer) he shuts his shop and goes to the mosque nearby with his three employees and within fifteen minutes he returns after the prayer, and reopens the shop. We found his shop the busiest in the market. We even see that when he shuts his shop at prayer time there is always a big queue waiting at the front of his shop, although other shops nearby are open. The other shops do not have half as many customers as this true Muslim. There are millions of examples, similar to this one, in the present world.

In a mosque in the USA a group of Islamic travellers, who were working on a project for the muslims, spent the night asleep. Their sound sleep made a neighbourhood police officer curious to know how they could enjoy such deep slumber. In reply to his question one of them explained to him, "You see, we never take sleeping pills as you are used to. We are Muslims, the followers of Islam, the core meaning of which is peace, the divine peace that is prescribed by Allah, the Providence of the universe. We abide by His holy words and consequently we inherit peace as His faithful servants". The police officer was charmed and asked them to show him the Qur'an. The leader gave him a copy of the Noble Book in translation with some admonitions.

However after a couple of days, the police officer appeared before the group with a certain look upon his face and in his manner. He explained that he had been receiving peace, both in mind and body, following the injunctions of the Qur'an and now he, with his entire family, had come to embrace Islam. "Please make us Muslims forthwith. We feel ourselves fortunate to have the sight of Islam just now. It is really a divine bliss upon us from Heaven, through you."

Britain's Daily Mail, dated December 2nd 1993, published an interview with four ladies who had embraced Islam. Some of them sighed at having been deprived for so long from coming in touch with Islam. "It seems to us that now we are at our genuine dwelling house."

Islam is neither a fiction nor a story. It is, as said earlier, the deen of nature, that is, the traits of human character are made by Allah Himself. Even the other creatures have to obey Allah according to the composition and size of their bodies and temperament. For them to follow Islam is binding and, in this same manner, every human being, irrespective of their wishes and whims, is a follower of Islam. In this sense, the cyclic order of birth, growth of the body and, ultimately, the death of every creature, is by nature already determined for all, and any deviation from this is not possible. It is because Allah is the creator of life, and hence the Lord of it, that He is the sole authority to give death.

However, Islam has been given to mankind as a complete guide, and it is by nature easy to follow and practice, provided man is sincerely committed to building up an honest, peaceful and prosperous life. In the noble Qur'an Allah says:

"Allah desires ease for you; He does not desire difficulty for you." (Surah 2: 184)

Again Allah says:

"Allah desires to make things lighter for you. Man was created weak." (Surah 4: 28)

The Creator knows well that His human creation is weak in all respects, and subject to love, anger, many conflicting emotions, greed, and so on and so forth. Again he is also equipped with the urge to do good even at the cost of his life. And such desires and convictions put man in conflicting situations and very often mislead him in taking the right and appropriate decisions. To save him from such riddles and dangers, he is given the noble Qur'an and the Sunnah for guidance both in spirit and in the everyday reality. Allah, the Merciful Himself helps him do good deeds in the right way. Allah says:

"He has made mercy incumbent on Himself." (Surah 6: 13)

The people who thus submit themselves sincerely to the will and command of Allah are called Muslims, and they are peace loving and peace keeping people, in mind and body, in life and society from the personal to the global level, in every way. The people who lead life in this manner, both in letter and spirit, will be awarded ascendancy and power over the globe. Allah says:

"Allah has promised those of you who have iman and do right actions that He will make them successors in the land as He made those before them successors, and will firmly establish for them their deen with which He is pleased and give them, in place of their fear, security. 'They worship Me, not associating anything with Me.'" (Surah 24: 55)

To lead life in an Islamic way certainly needs a conducive environment such as that in which the holy Prophet (SAAS) was seen. The life story of Muhammad (SAAS) is the greatest example for a Muslim to follow.

To attain this congenial atmosphere, the noble Qur'an commands the people of taqwa in the following words :

**"Instruct your family to do salat, and be constant in it. We do not ask you for provision. We provide for you. And the best end result is gained by taqwa." (Surah 20: 132)**

Prayer, i.e., salat in the proper sense also means a conscious process of purifying the self and body to attain perfection in words and deeds. In the Noble Qur'an it is said that in its true perspective and power salat prevents a man from doing anything obscene and immoral.

However in one hadith, our Prophet (SAAS) said that Allah says:

"O, son of Adam, stick to my worship, I shall fill your heart full of plenty and cast your poverty away. Otherwise, I shall make your heart entangled with complications, and then you will never be able to get out of poverty and satisfy yourself."

A true Muslim in fact is never worried for bread. He is so busy and devoted to serving Allah, that he has no time to think of earning. And for such a Muslim, Allah takes full responsibility to meet all his needs. As a result such a Muslim is found leading a bold and carefree life, never asking help of others. This glorious life he attains because he devotes his life and energy to the cause of making goodness flourish, by executing orders for doing good and prohibiting evils. He is thoroughly honest and without vanity, always forbearing and humane.

In the noble Qur'an Allah says:

**"You are the best nation ever to be produced before mankind. You enjoin the right, forbid the wrong and have iman in Allah." (Surah 3: 110)**

Why is it said so? It is simply because the Qur'an is for the welfare of the entire universe, not only for the Muslims, upon whom alone is the responsibility to establish goodness made incumbent. To wage war against evil, to institute a just society, is not dangerous to the Muslims in any way because Allah guarantees them safety, by saying:

> "Then when guidance comes to you from Me, those who follow My guidance will feel no fear and will know no sorrow." (Surah 2: 37)

Allah assures the people of taqwa more when He says in the Qur'an:

> "You who have iman! seek help in steadfastness and salat. Allah is with the steadfast." (Surah 2: 153)

He declares moreover:

> "Whoever has taqwa of Allah – He will give him a way out and provide for him from where he does not expect. Whoever puts his trust in Allah – He will be enough for him. Allah always achieves His aim. Allah has appointed a measure for all things." (Surah 65: 2-3)

In a hadith related by 'Umar, the Prophet (SAAS) said:

> "If you were to depend on Allah in the appropriate manner, Allah would certainly provide for you like He does for the birds and beasts wholeave their dwellings early in the morning with appetite, and come back in the evening with stomachs duly filled."

Allah is so much more merciful to man that He makes it evident by declaring:

> "We created man and We know what his own self whispers to him. We are nearer to him than his jugular vein." (Surah 50: 16)

Here a question may arise from the misunderstanding by Muslims of Islam: if every follower of Islam should be leading a happy life, are they, in fact, leading such happy lives in the present-day world? The answer would be –

no, not all of them, but at least some of them. The majority are suffering an oppressive life, for which there are many reasons. Many are in severe difficulties and yet are patient and true to Allah, so that those difficulties become easy for them, and they are sure that Allah will provide a way out of their difficulties. Some are Muslims in name only. They are not real Muslims, and can even be regarded as enemies of Islam, because they insult and humiliate Islam through not abiding by Islamic Laws, and not embracing Islam as a part of their human nature.

They embrace the evil aspects of nature and culture. According to history, Muslims ruled a great part of the world for several centuries, when they were true Muslims. Then the world was a peaceful paradise according to Islamic standards. As human beings, not only Muslims, if you do not act in accordance with your true human nature you are in danger. But these so-called Muslims, by not knowing or ignoring human nature, are out of harmony with it. For this they may have a double punishment. They are suffering at present: in the present-day world almost everybody is suffering (except a few true Muslims) from various disasters, physically, mentally, socially, politically, even in their families, because human beings are out of harmony with their human nature. But these so-called Muslims may suffer even more because they are humiliating and insulting the sacred nature on which they were created and also the revelation that they have which shows them how to live in accordance with their natural conditions.[1]

There are some true Muslims, living in prosperity and happiness even in the present world. Even if some of them are poor and in straitened circumstances, they are true to Allah and happy for what He has decreed for them, so that what would be difficult for others is easy for them. You can see them if you wish. They are living, actual examples of Islam.

---

[1] According to the Noble Qur'an man is superior to all other creatures, even the angels. So human nature is the highest nature possible, "Adorn yourselves with the attributes of Allah." Hadith.

# The miracle of the Qur'an

The last and final revealed message – the Noble Qur'an – is the su preme and, until the Last Day, the unique and unrivalled divine miracle for mankind. All branches of knowledge, concerning the past, present and future of the world, all that man needs to know about mind, body, matter, spirit, etc., are there in this Glorious Book. That is why all previous scriptures abrogated and outdated.

The first surah, "Fatihah", which consists of only seven ayat, embraces in a condensed manner all the teachings and admonitions of the entire Qur'an. The surah is therefore called *Ummu'l-Kitab*, "the core of the Book" for such riches and beauty as are expressed in these few terse words. The world-famous Islamic thinker Sheikh Mushahed Baiyam Puri made deliberations for seven long years on this surah and yet he could not explain half of it to his audience.

The celebrated French doctor, Dr. Mardress, was assigned the task of translating 62 surahs of the holy Qur'an into French, and this gave him the divine feeling and realisation of the meaning of the following. The art of expression of the Qur'an is certainly the evidence of the Creator's art of expression.

In the noble Qur'an Allah says:

> "Say: 'If both men and jinn banded together to produce the like of this Qur'an, they could never produce anything like it, even if they backed each other up.'" (Surah 17: 88)

The uniqueness and divinity of the Qur'an is thus without parallel to both mankind and the jinn, and this uniqueness and sublimity has made the sacred revelation an ever-shining miracle to man.

The greatness of the Qur'an lies in the following ayah, where Allah Himself proclaims:

**"It is We Who have sent down the Reminder and We Who will preserve it."** (Surah 15: 9)

The fundamentals of the creation of the universe, such as smoke (Nebula) being the first stage of the creation, the creation of the skies and the earth in six phases of time along with all other things that are essential for life to survive and be sustained as depicted in the Noble Qur'an are gradually revealing the scientific truth. The scientists of ages, past and present, as will those of the future, have been marching ahead to explore the Qur'an as the wisdom of Allah, the Lord, Sustainer and Judge of the worlds, known and yet to be known to mankind through the passage of time and space, the unbounding elements of the Creator. The shining stars in the sky are, for instance, ever-awe-inspiring phenomena of Allah, and they have been making man soar up and up to the spheres of Infinite Being, resulting in the discoveries of the numerous planets that seem to be striking elements of His unfathomable creation. What the last and final Prophet of Islam said over 1400 years ago about the 'Cosmos' and its divine Truth, is now proving to be fact, as the experiments of the scientists of the world overwhelmingly show.

The Noble Qur'an is, out and out, the Divine Book. The following appreciation of it, for instance, recently made by an American woman intellectual newly converted to Islam is noteworthy:

"How can I put into words the overwhelming relief that I feel when having discovered the answer to the questions I have been searching for all my life? It's like being blind and then suddenly given sight to a truth and a brightness never seen before. How can I tell of the joys that only finding the truth can bring? I want to sing it to the world. I want everyone I have ever known to share this with me and celebrate the door that has been opened to me. And the most wonderful and awesome thing shown to me was the glorious Qur'an. How I love and cherish my Qur'an! How I read it every chance I get! I cannot put it down! Even in English the words can bring joy to my heart and tears to my eyes! There have been many times when I held Allah's words in my hands and wept at the revelation. How could I have been such a fool all my life? I shudder to think of my life without Islam. If I could climb to the highest mountain and be heard by everyone who is blind to Islam, I would shout all that has been shown to me. My questions have been answered. I now know the truth. If every person in the world thanked Allah for bringing me the truth, one hundred times a day for one hundred years, that still would not express my gratitude." – Becky Hopkins (Islamic Horizons, December 1987, Bridge View, Illinois, USA.)

Here, in this context, a remark by the late Professor Arthur J. Arberry, a renowned English writer as well as researcher, is noteworthy. He was well-versed in Arabic and a translator of the Qur'an into English. He said: "Whenever I hear the Qur'an chanted, it is as though I am listening to music. Underneath the flowing melody there is sounding all the time the incessant beat of a drum. It is like the beating of my heart." Unfortunately, Professor Arberry, in spite of his translation of the Qur'an and some other great classics, never accepted Islam.

It is probably worthwhile properly dismissing one false 'scientific miracle' attributed to the Qur'an by a certain well known deviant from the deen. That is the so-called miracle of the number 19, a number which is mentioned by Allah in the following ayat of the Noble Qur'an:

**"What will convey to you what Saqar is? It does not spare and does not ease up, ceaselessly scorching the flesh. There are nineteen in charge of it. We have only appointed angels as masters of the Fire and We have only specified their number as a trial for those who are kafir; so that those who were given the Book might gain in certainty, and those**

who have iman might increase in their iman, and both those who were given the Book and the muminun might have no doubt; and so that those with sickness in their hearts and the kuffar might say, 'What did Allah intend by this example?' In this way Allah misguides those He wills and guides those He wills. No one knows the legions of your Lord but Him. This is nothing but a reminder to all human beings." (Surah 74: 27-31)

These ayat are the clearest proof against the false teaching that has circulated on the significance of the number 19 in the Qur'an – widely and mistakenly regarded by many muslims as a miracle of the Qur'an – because Allah says: "and so that those with sickness in their hearts and the kuffar might say, 'What did Allah intend by this example?'" showing that it is only people who are sick in their hearts and kuffar who investigate this matter. Moreover, He also says in Surah Al 'Imran, ayah 7:

"Those with deviation in their hearts follow what is open to interpretation in it (the Qur'an), desiring conflict, seeking its inner meaning. No one knows its inner meaning but Allah. Those firmly rooted in knowledge say, 'We have iman in it. All of it is from our Lord.'"

The matter concerning the number 19 is certainly one of the matters that is open to interpretation which it is thus deviation to enquire into.

Another towering personality is Dr. Maurice Bucaille whose *The Bible, The Qur'an and Science* has, of late, created a tremor in the hearts of modern educated people for its analytical and comparative studies of the subjects of its title. In his work Dr. Bucaille says that at the beginning he was surprised when going through the specific matters of science mentioned in the Noble Qur'an. After close study, he came to the firm conclusion that it was not at all possible for a human being alone to find out the meaning and connotation of the scientific terms expressed in the Qur'an. He was amazed to see that all the sciences told of in the Qur'an are, with the passage of time and scientific discovery and invention, proving to be true.

He points out that Westerners always try to identify Muslims as Mohammedans with a view to making them appear the worshippers of the cult of Muhammad (SAAS) instead of recognising them as those who practise Islam. Their motive is to brand Muslims as the followers of a person, but not practitioners of Islam, the divine code of life. This trick had, Dr. Bucaille says, led him to be confused about Islam, as a teaching for mankind, and prevented him for a long time from recognising the true light.

However, Allah's blessing was on him, for Dr. Bucaille got the opportunity to meet the late King Faisal, "who did enlighten me regarding the erroneous opinions the West has towards Islam", and for this guidance, he expresses deep gratitude to the late King and implores Allah for peace for the departed King's soul. This new light from the King led Dr. Bucaille to develop an intense desire to learn Arabic, and this has him adept in studying Arab literature, and conducting enquiries into the Noble Qur'an in a proper way. Being thus equipped with knowledge of Qur'an, he made comparative studies of it and the Bible and found out that while the Bible is much distorted and altered, both in contents and structure, the Noble Qur'an, since its revelation, has survived untarnished both in form and content, in absolute perfection, beauty and honour. This awed him profoundly. He wrote, "The humanist interpretation of the Noble Qur'an (Qur'an) in any way or form is quite impossible," and "the Qur'an is not the creation of man, rather it is, indeed, a revealed Scripture from Heaven."

In his book Dr. Bucaille stated that, "These scientific considerations, which are very specific to the Qur'an, greatly surprised me at first. Up until then, I had not thought it possible for one to find so many statements in a text compiled more than thirteen centuries ago referring to extremely diverse subjects and all of them totally in keeping with modern scientific knowledge. In the beginning, I had no faith whatsoever in Islam. I began this examination of the texts with a completely open mind and a total objectivity. If there was any influence acting upon me, it was gained from what I had been taught in my youth; people did not speak of Muslims, but of 'Mohammedans', to make it quite clear that what was meant was a religion founded by a man and which could not therefore have any kind of value in terms of God. Like many in the West, I could have retained the same false notions about Islam; they are so widespread today, that I am indeed surprised when I come across anyone, other than a specialist, who can talk in an enlightened manner on this subject. I therefore admit that before I was given a view of Islam different from the one received in the West, I was myself extremely ignorant.

"I owe the fact that I was able to realise the false nature of the judgements generally made in the West about Islam to exceptional circumstances. It was in Saudi Arabia itself that an inkling was given to me of the extent to which opinions held in the West on this subject are liable to error.

"The debt of gratitude I owe to the late King Faisal, whose memory I salute with deepest respect, is indeed very great: the fact that I was given the signal honour of hearing him speak on Islam and was able to raise with him certain problems concerning the interpretation of the Qur'an in relation to modern science is a very cherished memory. It was an extremely great privilege for me to have gathered so much precious information from him personally and those around him.

"Since I had now seen the wide gap separating the reality of Islam from the image we have of it in the West, I experienced a great need to learn Arabic (which I did not speak) to be sufficiently well-equipped to progress in the study of such a misunderstood religion. My first goal was to read the Qur'an and to make a sentence-by-sentence analysis of it with the help of various commentaries essential to a critical study. My approach was to pay special attention to the description of numerous natural phenomena given in the Qur'an; the highly accurate nature of certain details referring to them in the Book, which was only apparent in the original, struck me by the fact that they were in keeping with present-day ideas, although a man living at the time of Muhammad could not have suspected this at all. I subsequently read several works written by Muslim authors on the scientific aspects of the Qur'anic text: they were extremely helpful in my appreciation of it, but I have not so far discovered a general study of this subject made in the West.

"What initially strikes the reader confronted for the first time with a text of this kind is the sheer abundance of subjects discussed: the Creation, astronomy, the explanation of certain matters concerning the earth, and the animal and vegetable kingdoms, human reproduction. Whereas monumental errors are to be found in the Bible, I could not find a single error in the Qur'an. I had to stop and ask myself: If a man was the author of the Qur'an, how could he have written facts in the Seventh century AD that today are shown to be in keeping with modern scientific knowledge? There was absolutely no doubt about it: the text of the Qur'an we have today is most definitely a text of the period, if I may be allowed to put it in these terms. What human explanation can there be to this observation? In my opinion there is no explanation; there is no special reason why an inhabitant of the Arabian Peninsula should, at a time when King Dagobert was reigning in France (629-639 AD), have had scientific knowledge on certain subjects that was ten centuries ahead of our own.

"It is an established fact that at the time of the Qur'anic Revelation, i.e. within a period of roughly twenty years straddling Hijrah (622 AD), scientific knowledge had not progressed for centuries and the period of activity in Islamic civilisation, with its accompanying scientific upsurge, came after the close of the Qur'anic Revelation. Only ignorance of such religious and secular data can lead to the following bizarre suggestion I have heard several times: if surprising statements of a scientific nature exist in the Qur'an, they may be accounted for by the fact that Arab scientists were far ahead of their time and Muhammad was influenced by their work. Anyone who knows anything about Islamic history is aware that the period of the Middle Ages which saw the cultural and scientific upsurge in the Arab world came after Muhammad and would not therefore indulge in such whims. Suggestions of this kind are particularly off the mark in that the majority of scientific facts which are either suggested or very clearly recorded in the Qur'an have only been confirmed in modern times." (The Bible, the Qur'an and Science, pages 128-129)

Dr. Bucaille concluded that "In view of the state of knowledge in Muhammad's day, it is inconceivable that many of the statements in the Qur'an, which are connected with science, could have been the work of a man. It is, moreover, perfectly legitimate not only to regard the Qur'an as the expression of a Revelation, but also to award it a very special place on account of the guarantee of authenticity it provides and the presence in it of scientific statements which, when studied today, appear as a challenge to human explanation." (*The Bible, the Qur'an and Science*, page 269)

The next question which comes to mind is: why is the Qur'an revealed in Arabic? The plain and uncritical answer might be that, in words attributed to the Prophet (SAAS): "I love the Arabs for three reasons: My tongue is Arabic, the Noble Qur'an is in Arabic and the language of the inhabitants of Heavens is Arabic." However, this hadith is regarded as a fabricated hadith by the scholars of hadith. However, a study of Arabic shows that it is little affected by other religions and cultures, such as Judaism and Christianity, or Persian, Greek or Roman culture. Thus the meanings of Arabic are close to the *fitrah* – to the natural condition of the human being. In other languages, the meanings have been changed by the old religions and philosophies of the people which have become decadent and corrupted. When the Qur'an was revealed Arabic was free of this corruption, and Allah knows best.

Thus it is apparent why Arabic has been chosen for the Qur'an, and how much the loftiness of this language has been bestowed divinely upon it. In addition to it this language is now the mother tongue of as many as 38 countries, in which the use and preservation of its grammar and syntax automatically, and even unconsciously, safeguards the practice of the Qur'an in daily rites and regular practices of the deen. Therefore, the foes of Islam are unable to deform and decry this revelation because of Allah's undertaking the responsibility to guard and protect it miraculously.

The infidels and enemies of Islam used to stigmatise Islam, claiming it achieved its ascendancy over the world by dint of the sword and power. This is a lie and a heinous conspiracy to undo the beauty and glory of Islam, the benign gift of Allah to the entire world.

In the Qur'an Allah says:

> "There is no compulsion where the deen is concerned. Right guidance has become clearly distinct from error. Anyone who rejects false gods[1] and has iman in Allah has grasped the Firmest Handhold, which will never give way. Allah is All-Hearing, All-Knowing." (Surah 2: 256)

> "You have your deen and I have my deen." (Surah 109: 6)

> "You who have iman! show integrity for the sake of Allah, bearing witness with justice. Do not let hatred for a people incite you into not being just. Be just. That is closer to taqwa. Have taqwa of Allah. Allah is aware of what you do." (Surah 5: 8)

> "We did not appoint you over them as their keeper and you are not set over them as their guardian." (Surah 6: 108)

All these ayat made the Prophet (SAAS) and his following play a decisive role, even at critical moments, in fighting his deadly enemies, who imposed upon the Muslims the fiery battles of Badr, Uhud and the Ditch. Moreover the Prophet's (SAAS) dealing with the captives of war, his treaties with enemies, his patience with his deadly enemies – all these transparently belie the allegations of the anti-Islamic world as lies intended to undermine the glory of the Qur'an, and its Lord Allah with His Prophet Muhammad (SAAS). History upholds this truth until the final Day of Judgement!

### On Fundamentalism

The term 'Fundamentalism' is from the word 'Fundamental' which means "of or forming the basis or foundation", or it means "of very great importance". Hence fundamentalism means practice of, and advocacy for, funda-

---

[1] The word *Taghut* (here translated as "false gods") covers a wide range of meanings. It means anything worshipped other than the real God, Allah.

mentals or foundations of any thing or belief. The staunch followers of such fundamentals are known as fundamentalists.

Fundamentalism was religious movement among some US Protestants, which started after World War I. It insisted on the literal truth of the Bible and of such traditional teachings as the Virgin Birth and Christ rising bodily from the dead. It rejected scientific knowledge, such as the theory of evolution, that does not agree with the Bible.

However, the same invective term has recently been imported into our religious arena by intellectually servile miscreants, to cunningly attempt to tarnish the power and glory of Islam.

The enemies of Islam, living outside the Muslim world, are now banking on the support of already powerful, indigenous agents, by offering high degrees in universal knowledge and education that are, in the true sense, an act of alienation from Islamic teaching. They offer this in the guise of university education, consisting usually of elements of Epicurean thought and culture. Wise people in society have realized the gravity of this situation and, therefore, devoted themselves to the Muslim Ummah (society). This has gradually been gaining ground, in power and popularity all over the world. Foreign and indigenous foes of Islam have played the role, in the imputation of fundamentalism, of slandering and opposing the fighting spirit of the Muslim reformers of the world. By promises of money, of economy, of culture and recently of religion, they have made their agents, so-called intellectuals, wage war against Islam, fighting in the field of secular education, politics, the economy and social surroundings.

These agents have been well educated in anti-Islamic knowledge through so-called school, college and university educations that are nursing the poisonous seedling plants and trees to make the learner eat the fruits of the forbidden trees, and to expel them from the jurisdiction of Islam. This is being done in the name of universal and humanitarian education virtually compelling them towards a godlessness evident in both their intellects and manners.

Consequently the Muslims who have been cursed in this way are now working against the Qur'an, the Sunnah and Islamic Tawhid. They are now being dextrously manipulated, financed, empowered, guided and pushed by their anti-Islamic masters. They have been renaming Muslims, by adding fundamentalist as a pejorative term to their Islamic words and deeds. They call them 'Fundamentalists' to make people treat them as the fanatical anti-intellectual and anti-scientific Protestant sects. What shaytans they are!

Thus the committed enemies of Islam have successfully been creating factions and friction among them, contradictions and collisions among the students of Islamic Universities. The result is now apparent. So-called modern Muslims now assert Islam as a personal matter that has nothing to do with state politics, legislation, economics and so on.

As a result, all physical and material power and resources of the mundane world have come under the control and dictation of secular authorities. They have almost made the majority of people, especially the Muslims, alienated from belief in Qiyamah – the Day of Rising from the dead – nay, the Eternal world where human beings, along with jinn, shall have immortality to suffer severe pains, or enjoy undiminishing and ever-new pleasures, in accordance with the deeds, bad or goods, that they have done here on this mortal planet.

### As-Sa'ah – the Last Hour of the world

In several pages of the Noble Qur'an, Allah warns that the evildoers will be punished, and the people of taqwa rewarded, after weighing their deeds, good and bad, in detail and meticulously.

Here it would in no way be either redundant or inappropriate to quote scientists' remarks that act as some kind of evidence of the reality of the Last Hour of the world, about which the Noble Qur'an has already given the verdict.

Scientists have recently come to the firm conviction that in the vast space of heaven there are innumerable stars comprising the galaxy of the Milky Way, some of which are so vast that each of them comprises millions of stars. They further assert that the sun we see now shall one day collapse and then become a Red Giant star destroying the entire solar system, and that it is very possible that the entire universe will collapse in on itself. These remarks are no less fantastic than the divine truth the Qur'an has already declared over 1400 years ago in the following ayat:

Surat at-Takwir – The Compacting

In the name of Allah, All-Merciful, Most Merciful

When the sun is compacted in blackness,

when the stars fall in rapid succession,

when the mountains are set in motion,

when the camels in foal are neglected,

when the wild beasts are all herded together,

when the oceans surge into each other,

when the selves are arranged into classes,

when the baby girl buried alive is asked

for what crime she was killed,

when the Pages are opened up,

when the Heaven is peeled away,

when the Fire is set ablaze,

when the Garden is brought up close:

then will each self know what it has done.

No! I swear by the planets with their retrograde motion,

swiftly moving, self-concealing,

and by the night when it draws in,

and by the dawn when it exhales,

truly it is the speech of a noble Messenger,

possessing great strength,

securely placed with the Lord of the Throne,

obeyed there, trustworthy.

(Surah at-Takwir: 1-21)

However, woe to those who have wickedly engaged themselves in sullying the divine message of the love of Allah and His Prophet (SAAS), despite science's corroboration of the contents of the Qur'an, every moment of time!

Let us conclude this chapter quoting the celebrated historian Arnold J. Toynbee, who in his work *Civilization on Trial* has vividly upheld the essence of Islam as the only panacea to all sorts of modern ills and to the long sighing of modernists already gone astray:

"We can, however, discern principles of Islam which, if brought to bear on the social life of the new cosmopolitan proletariat, might have important salutary effects on 'the great society' in a nearer future. Two conspicuous sources of danger – one psychological and the other material – in the present relations of this cosmopolitan proletariat with the dominant element in our modern Western society are race consciousness and alcohol; and in the struggle with each of these evils the Islamic spirit has a service to render which might prove, if it were accepted, to be of high moral and social value.

"The extinction of race consciousness as between Muslims, is one of the outstanding moral achievements of Islam, and in the contemporary world there is, as it happens, crying need for the propagation of this Islamic value."

# Qiyamah – the Day of Rising

## in the light of the Qur'an and science

S ome people are suspicious about the Day of Rising because they do not believe in anything without seeing or feeling it, although if they use their brains and look at themselves and nature they will clearly see with their inner eyes. Science today tells us that this universe will be destroyed one day. And Allah says in the Noble Qur'an:

> "It is He who created you from clay and then decreed a fixed term, and another fixed term is specified with Him. Yet you still have doubts!" (Surah 6: 2)

Here man is told that his self, his existence is a kind of small world. If you think about it's beginning, living and consequence, then the Oneness of Allah and the Day of Rising will become a real truth apparent to you. There are two consequences to this life. One is personal, which is the death of a man. The other concerns all men, and the death of the universe, which is as-Sa'ah or the Last Hour when everything will be destroyed, after which man will be resurrected. The personal consequence of this life is the death of a man at his decreed term: on that date he will die. Man does not know that date, but he knows that he will die one day. The consequence for the universe is that it has a decreed term for death (i.e. to be destroyed), but nobody knows that date except its Creator, Allah All-mighty.

So, the death of a man is his personal Sa'ah or Last Hour, when he leave his body in the earth to be destroyed. This is a plain indication of the Last Hour of the world.

The existence of man has two parts. One is matter and the other is spirit. Matter is the body, which will be destroyed and vanish in the earth. The spirit is the soul which is immortal. Everybody knows that the soul is the original existence of a man. If there is no soul, there is nobody. But if there is a soul, a body can be built, as it is built in a mother's womb. The matter, the body, is made from clay, and this is how: we eat foods which are grown from clay, the ground, this body grew from the goodness of foods from the earth, then by this body, with sexual discharge (semen) a human body is made in a woman's womb. This discharge is the essence of clay. This is how the body is originally made from clay. In the noble Qur'an Allah says:

> "He who has created all things in the best possible way. He commenced the creation of man from clay; then produced his seed from an extract of base fluid; then formed him and breathed His Ruh into him and gave you hearing, sight and hearts. What little thanks you show!" (Surah 32: 6-8)

The Ruh (soul) is the original man, direct from its Creator, Allah, the All-mighty. Again Allah says in the noble Qur'an:

> "We created man from the purest kind of clay; then made him a drop in a secure receptacle; then formed the drop into a clot and formed the clot into a lump and formed the lump into bones and clothed the bones in flesh; and then brought him into being as another creature. Blessed be Allah, the Best of Creators!" (Surah 23: 12-14)

Now, the soul (original man) is sense within the body, and drives and directs it. The body does not have its own sense. It's made of clay, so when the soul (original man) leaves the body, it vanishes in clay, or soil and dust, and the atoms of the body are mixed in the dust of the earth, whether the body is buried, burnt or dropped in the ocean. After the whole Universe is destroyed before the Last Day, the creator Allah will create a vast land – much larger than this earth – and from that land all men's bodies will rise when Allah commands the souls to return to their bodies to be resurrected for the final judgement and the eternal life thereafter.

### Rising from the Dead
When we were in the wombs of our mothers, then that was our world for a

few months. We were living then in comfort and peace. At that time if we were told that we were going to enter a world that was much, much larger and more comfortable, and that we would have to live on this world called earth for a very much longer time than we had spent in the womb, it would have seemed unbelievable. But that has already happened through our being born here.

Everything is possible to our All-mighty Creator Allah. Once we were born from the wombs of our mothers, and we will be born again from the womb of the soil. That is our other birth into eternal life. Our births and deaths are departures only. We have given them different names, birth and death, but actually they are the same. The only difference is that we are born here on this earth as children to gain knowledge and to test our greatness as human beings, and we will be reborn then as adults to face the consequences, to suffer or to gain. In the noble Qur'an Allah says:

**"We made everything on the earth adornment for it so that we could test them to see whose actions are the best. We will certainly make everything on it a barren wasteland." (Surah 18: 7-8)**

In the noble Qur'an, on the means to have a better and peaceful life here and to win in the judgement on Day of Reckoning, Allah says:

**"Those who respond to their Lord will receive the best." (Surah 13:20)**

> **"When the Great Event occurs,**
>
> **none will deny its occurrence;**
>
> **bringing low, raising high.**
>
> **When the earth is convulsed**
>
> **and the mountains are crushed**
>
> **and become scattered dust in the air.**

And you will be classed into three:

the Companions of the Right:

what of the Companions of the Right?

the Companions of the Left:

what of the Companions of the Left?

and the Forerunners,

the Forerunners.

Those are the Ones Brought Near

in Gardens of Delight." (Surah 56: 1-14)

"Today no self will be wronged in any way. You will only be repaid for what you did. The Companions of the Garden are busy enjoying themselves today." (Surah 36: 53-54)

"They will be paraded before your Lord in ranks: 'You have come to Us just as We created you at first. Yes indeed! Even though you claimed that We would not fix a time with you.' The Book will be set in place and you will see the evildoers fearful of what is in it. They will say, 'Alas for us! What is this Book which does not pass over any action, small or great, without recording it?' They will find there everything they did and your Lord will not wrong anyone at all." (Surah 18: 47-48)

"'Keep yourselves apart today, you evildoers! Did I not make a contract with you, tribe of Adam, not to worship Shaytan, who truly is an outright enemy to you, but to worship Me? That is a straight path. He has led huge numbers of you into error. Why did you not use your intellect? This is the Hell that you were promised. Roast in it today because you were kafirun.' Today We seal up their mouths and their hands speak to us, and their feet bear witness to what they have earned." (Surah 36: 58-64)

"It has been revealed to you and those before you:

'If you associate others with Allah,

your actions will come to nothing

and you will be among the losers.'

No! Worship Allah and be among the thankful.

They do not measure Allah with His true measure.

The whole earth will be a mere handful

for Him on the Day of Rising,

the heavens folded up in His right hand.

Glory be to Him!

He is exalted above the partners they ascribe!

The Trumpet will be blown

and those in the heavens

and those in the earth

will all lose consciousness,

except those Allah wills.

Then it will be blown a second time

and at once they will be standing upright,

looking on.

And the earth will shine with the Pure Light of its Lord;

the Book will be put in place;

the Prophets and witnesses will be brought;

it will be decided between them with the truth;

and they will not be wronged.

Every self will be repaid in full for what it did.

He knows best what they are doing.

Those who are kafir will be driven to Hell in companies

and when they arrive there and its gates are opened

its custodians will say to them,

'Did Messengers from yourselves not come to you,

reciting your Lord's Signs to you and warning you

of the meeting on this Day of yours?'

They will say, 'Indeed they did, but the decree of punishment

is justly carried out against the kafirun.'" (Surah 39: 62-68)

"It is He who gave you life and then will cause you to die and then will give you life again. Man is truly ungrateful." (Surah 22: 64)

# Conclusion

In accordance with all the reasoning of psychology, philosophy, science and history, all the proofs of reality, we therefore conclude that Islam is the religion of human nature, from Allah the Creator.

Men who are looking for their God have found Him, but only through Islam. And only they live in this world with peace and prosperity. They have nothing to worry about, nor are they ever without hope.

No-one has found his God without Islam. Islam means submission to Allah, and another meaning stems from peace and tranquillity. Submission to Allah is the only way of peace and tranquillity. Only the Creator knows what is good and bad for His creature. The creature should follow His dictates with submission. And this is only the nature of creation. If a creature goes against its nature, that creature will be in danger. In analysing the word 'nature' a quotation from a distinguished Western philosopher is to be noted here: "Submission to the God is the only religion for both Man and Universe." So the meaning of Islam is submission to Allah, and this is in accordance with 'nature'.

It has been proved that only Islam can establish peace in the world, personally, socially and globally.

The religion of nature should be the nature of man, or else man is in danger. And this is the present situation in the world. We have done so much in modern science and civilisation to obtain some peace in our day-to-day lives, yet we are failing to attain such peace. Day by day we are even getting into a worse situation in our lives. Although science is part of our nature, we, ourselves, are becoming unnatural. We are out of touch with our own natures – Islam, as submission to Allah. Today, although men are living with nature, they themselves are unnatural. If you have forgotten your nature, you have forgotten your Creator, your God. Thus there is no peace and tranquillity, either personally, socially or globally, except for a few fortunate, true Muslims.

By forgetting your own nature you have also forgotten and are ignorant of your own self. You do not know what the spiritual power is within you, when you are in your own nature, that the whole universe is ready to serve you fully and promptly.

Here is a quotation from a famous Western philosopher, who wrote: "It is a question for us now to consider whether we have any personal relations towards the supreme power: whether there exists another world in which we shall be requited according to our actions. Not only is this a grand problem of philosophy, it is of all questions the most practical for us, the one in which our interests are most vitally concerned. This life is short, and its pleasures are poor: when we have obtained what we desire it is nearly time to die. If it can be shown that by living in a certain manner, eternal happiness may be obtained, then clearly no one except a fool or a madman will refuse to live in such a manner." That manner, i.e. nature, indeed is Islam, from here to the Garden.

As a materialist, please go and see the lifestyle of true Muslims. You will ask yourself with surprise, "How can a person live a life with such tranquillity and prosperity!"

# Muhammad (SAAS) – the last Prophet of Islam

Muhammad ibn 'Abdullah, the last and final Prophet (SAAS) of Islam is singularly a man unique and unparalleled in kindness and generosity. All the noblest qualities such as courtesy, honesty, patience, bravery, uprightness, benevolence, forgiveness, etc., were the traits of his most sublime, character.

When he had with him any surplus wealth or riches, he could not have peace of mind until it been bestowed upon some deserving person. He was so simple and painstaking, so benevolent and graceful that he often had to spend his days in distress and hunger. He used to mend his own shoes, and aid his family in doing petty household chores almost every day. He had absolutely no pride or vanity in his soul, and therefore was seen to accept the requests, even of the slaves, with whole heart and satisfaction.

Never did he show rage against anyone for any wound or offence done to him. Nor was he seen to take revenge upon anyone for his own sake. Hence we see even his deadly enemies enjoy the continuation of their lives after they had committed unpardonable crimes. Rather he asked for their forgiveness. The horrific incident of Ta'if, for instance, is one of the best citations to show him as the *Rahmatu'l-li'l-'Alameen*[1] or the "Blessing upon the universe" in reality.

He always absolutely and devotedly depended on Allah for his life and existence. That is why he had even gone amongst his enemies without bodyguards and personal attendants. Very often he used to go on foot to attend to everyday duties and calls. Excessive laughter as a means to express fun or

---

[1] In the noble Qur'an Allah describes the Prophet Muhammad (SAAS) with these words.

joy was foreign to his nature, although he was full of joy. He participated in competitive foot-races with some of his wives. For recreation, sometimes, walking with his companions was his pleasure.

Muhammad (SAAS) the last Messenger of Allah was untutored. That had been so that he would fulfil the Divine Will. To be literate is to read something written by someone who is by nature not perfect in thought nor character. If Muhammad had read, then his sublime innocence of character and its uprightness in thought and manner would have been influenced and biased. To keep him free of such tendencies and stigmas his heart had, more than once, been purified by angels from heaven, and he had, in the cave of Hira, been taught divine knowledge by Allah Himself, through His messenger Jibril (AS), who said:

**"Recite: In the Name of your Lord who created."** Muhammad the untutored, then and there become enlightened. Jibril later said to him:

"O Muhammad! you are Allah's messenger, and I am Jibril." Thenceforth, he became the teacher of mankind. In his words *"Bu'ithtu Mu'allima –* I have been sent as the teacher [to you]."

He had always been the first in offering greetings of peace to anyone, disregarding age and gender. Whoever used to meet him, had the feeling of the Prophet (SAAS) showing him great honour and respect. He sometimes spread his cloak as a seat for his guests and visitors. His words were sweet and concise, straight and unambiguous, and pleasant to the ears and soul. When he walked, he walked steadily, and made no sound in stepping, but moved alertly. He would take simple, ordinary meals and say:

"I am simply a slave. I take my food like a slave taking his." He did not like a rich diet, nor had he any attachment to luxuries. He preferred warm dishes to cold ones. Grapes and water melon were among his favourites. He used to take dates and water as regular food and drink. Sometimes he drank milk mixed with dates. Meat was a much liked by him. He used to say:

"Meat enhances the power of hearing, and it is, of all foods, the best. If I would implore my Lord for meat as my daily food, He would surely award me it."

Another favourite was the gourd. He used to say, "The gourd was my brother Yunus' fruit." He asked his accomplished wife A'ishah (RA), "When you cook meat, cook it with much gourd, because it strengthens the heart." Vinegar, salad and water sweetened by honey, were also favourite items of food and drink.

He took one meal a day, and never had it while anybody went hungry, to his knowledge. After having his meals he expressed profound gratitude to Allah, the Holy Being,

"Oh Lord! All praises belong to you. You have provided food, bestowed satisfaction and given water," and thus he ever humbled his self before Him.

He allowed none to praise him and when he called on anyone at his house he used to stand at the right side of the door and greet the owner of the house. He did it to preserve the dignity of the veil of the womenfolk inside the house. He used perfume frequently and green and white were the colours of dress much to his liking. He had an embroidered mantle. As headdress he put on a cap and sometimes turban. Most of his clothes were white and when he had new clothes, he wore them first on Friday for regular use and he made a gift of the old clothes. He used to put a silver ring on his finger. His bed was a mat, with a pillow of leather filled with date-fibre. Muhammad (SAAS) was neither too tall nor too short, but between these extremes. When he walked, he seemed to be of medium stature, but, with great surprise, when he walked with tall people, he seemed to be taller than these individuals. He had a fair and glorious complexion, but that does not mean that it had too much either of whiteness, or reddish brown. The complexion of his person had the mixed hue of the colours red and white together. His sweat-drops reflected like pearls, from which the smell of perfume, like Meshk saffron, used to emanate. His hair was exquisitely beautiful, neither very straight nor very curly; it reached his shoulder, or to the ends of his ears. His neck was as brilliant as pearls, cheeks wide and perfectly smooth. Between both his eyebrows his eyes were silvery dazzling, with lovely charm. His eyes were wide and oblong, nose narrow but not long, teeth well formed and marvellously beautiful to look at. When he used to laugh and smile, his teeth sparkled like lightning. His lips were supreme in beauty, his beard was most beautiful for its density and shape. His chest was broad, plain and had a golden moon-colour. His shoulders were broad and furnished with some beautiful hairs and the 'seal of Prophethood' shone between them. This mark he had from birth. It was a black and yellow spot of mixed colour, around which some hairs emitted a unique beauty. His arms and hands were fleshy, fingers as beautiful as silvery sticks. If he touched anyone's head with his palm, that head could be identified because of the influence of that hand's touch.

The Prophet (SAAS) used to say about himself, "I have much likeness to Adam (SAAS) in respect of the structure of body, and in respect of the character I have much likeness to that of Ibrahim (AS)."

Our Prophet was the bravest and boldest of all the brave and bold warriors that have ever been. The battle of Badr shows him the best: his acumen, sagacity and martial art, by dint of which he had inflicted a severe defeat upon his deadly enemies, three times greater in manpower, armaments and equipment than those of his own. Again, he is the best, the supreme completely unparalleled ruler the world has ever seen, and for this uniqueness of character, and his sacrifices, he is the model of human life, society and civilisation for all time, until the Last Day.

Allah Himself has praised our Prophet (SAAS) in the Qur'an, saying of him that he is an "*Uswah hasanah*" (an excellent model) for mankind until the great destruction of all creation.

# Postscript:
# Islam is human nature

Here are some quotations from some of the world's most distinguished converts to Islam:

"'Every child is born with a disposition towards the natural religion of obedience (i.e. Islam); it is the parents who make him a Jew, a Christian or a Magian.' – a saying of Muhammad (SAAS). Having been born in Islam it was a good many years before I realised this fact..."

William Burchell Bashir Pickard (England)
Author, poet and novelist

"In becoming a Muslim I have merely obeyed the dictates of my conscience, and have since felt a better and a truer man."

Sir Abdullah Archibald Hamilton (England)
Statesman and Baronet

"As a Doctor of Medicine, and a descendant of a French Catholic family, the very choice of my profession had given me a solid scientific culture which had prepared me very little for mystic life. Not that I did not believe in God, but that the dogmas and rites of Christianity in general, and of Catholicism in particular, never permitted me to feel His presence...

"Without yet knowing Islam I was already believing in the first part of the Kalimah, LA ILAHA IL-LAL-LAH (There is but one God)...

"Another point which moved me away from Christianity is the absolute silence which it maintains regarding bodily cleanliness, particularly before prayers, which has always seemed to me to be an outrage against God. For if He has given us a soul, He has also given us a body, which we have no right to neglect. The same silence could be observed, and this time mixed with hostility, with regard to the physiological life of the human being, whereas on this point Islam seemed to me to be the only religion in accord with human nature."

Ali Selman Benoist (France)

Doctor of Medicine

"Why do Westerners embrace Islam? There are various reasons for it. In the first place truth has always its force. The basic tenets of Islam are so rational, so natural and so appealing that an honest truth-seeker cannot help being impressed by them.

"I have lived under different systems of life and have had the opportunity of studying various ideologies, but have come to the conclusion that none is as perfect as Islam."

Muhammad Aman Hobohm (Germany)

Diplomat, missionary and social worker

"I have now but a little time to live upon this earth and I mean to devote my all to Islam."

Sir Jalaluddin Lauder Brunton (England)

Baronet and a public man of wide repute

"Islam supplemented my own ideas by some of the most ingenious conceptions of mankind ever thought of. The belief in God is something sacred to the religion of Islam. But it does not proclaim dogmas which are incompatible with modern science. Therefore there are no conflicts between belief on the one hand and science on the other. This fact is naturally a unique and enormous advantage for a man who participated to the best of his ability in scientific research. The second advantage is that the religion of Islam is not an idealistic teaching which runs along blindly beside life as it is, but that it preaches a system which actually influences the life of a human being … the laws of Islam are not compulsory regulations, which restrict personal freedom, but directions and guides which enable a well-contrived freedom.

"Throughout the years I have noticed time and again, with deepest satisfaction, that Islam holds the golden mean between individualism and socialism, between which it forms a connecting link. As it is unbiased and tolerant, it always appreciates the good, wherever it may happen to come across it."

Dr. Hamid Marcus (Germany)
Scientist, author and journalist

"We in the West find it difficult to acquaint ourselves with Islam, for since the days of the Christian Crusades there has been either a conspiracy of silence or a deliberate perversion of Islamic matters. Anyway, at the time living in Australia, I asked for a copy of the Noble Qur'an at the Sydney Public Library. When I was given the Book and was reading the preface by the translator, the bigotry against Islam was so obvious that I closed it up. There was no Qur'an translated by a Muslim available. Some weeks later in Perth, Western Australia, I again asked at the library for a copy of the Qur'an, stipulating that the translator must be a Muslim. It is difficult to put into words my immediate response to the first Surah, the seven opening verses. Then I read something of the life of the Prophet (Peace be upon him). I spent hours in the library that day. I had found what I wanted, by the mercy of Allah. I was a Muslim. I had not at this time met any Muslim. I came out of the library that day exhausted by the tremendous intellectual and emotional experience I had received. The next experience, I still ask myself: was it true or was it something I had dreamed up, for in cold print it seems impossible to have happened. I came out of the library intending to get myself a cup of coffee. I walked down the street and raising my eyes to a building beyond a high brick wall, I saw the words 'Muslim Mosque'. I straightaway said to myself 'You know the truth, now accept it'.

"'LA ILAHA IL-LAL-LAH MUHAMMADUR RASULUL-LAH' and so by the mercy of Allah I became a Muslim."

Muhammad John Webster (England)
President, the English Muslim Mission

"I have found Islam to be congenial to my mind and to the ideology in which I was educated in my infancy. I have found in Islam a perfect and complete code of life, which code is able to guide the individual and community towards the Kingdom of God on earth, and which is elastic enough to be adapted to modern conditions."

Ismail Wieslaw Zejierski (Poland)

Sociologist, reformer and social worker

"I am often asked when and why I became a Muslim. I can only reply that I do not know the precise moment when the truth of Islam dawned upon me. It seems that I have always been a Muslim. This is not so strange when one remembers that Islam is the natural religion that a child, left to itself, would develop. Indeed as a Western critic once described it, 'Islam is the religion of common sense'."

Lady Evelyn Zeinab Cobbold (England)

"I like the Muslim way of life which is pure, simple and essentially peaceful. I am convinced that Islam alone can bring peace in an individual's way of life as well as in the collective life of Man. Islam alone can give real peace to mankind – a peace which humanity is eager to have. I am happy to have acquired this peace and would like to spread Islam as much as possible amongst my people."

Miss Fatima Kazue (Japan)

"Why did I embrace Islam? First and foremost I would say it was because fundamentally I had always been a Muslim without being aware of it."

Mrs. Cecilia Mahmuda Connolly (Australia)

### Sayings of some of the world's most famous people

"I have always held the religion of Muhammad in high estimation because of its wonderful vitality. It is the only religion which ap-pears to me to possess that assimilating capacity to the changing phase of existence which can make itself appeal to every age. I have studied him – the

85

wonderful man, and in my opinion far from being an anti-Christ, he must be called the saviour of Humanity. I believe that if a man like him were to assume the dictatorship of the modern world, he would succeed in solving its problems in a way that would bring it the much-needed peace and happiness: I have prophesied about the faith of Muhammad, that it would be acceptable to the Europe of tomorrow as it is beginning to be acceptable to the Europe of today."

George Bernard Shaw,
(*The Genuine Islam*, Singapore, Vol. 1, No. 8)

"Our use of the phrase 'The Dark Ages' to cover the period from 699 to 1,000 marks our undue concentration on Western Europe... From India to Spain, the brilliant civilisation of Islam flourished. What was lost to Christendom at this time was not lost to civilisation, but quite the contrary... To us it seems that West-European civilisation is civilisation, but this is a narrow view."

Bertrand Russell
(*History of Western Philosophy*, London, p419)

"Why should we be surprised at this when we know that, for Islam, religion and science have always been considered twin sisters? From the very beginning, Islam directed people to cultivate science; the application of this precept brought with it the prodigious strides in science taken during the great era of Islamic civilisation, from which, before the Renaissance, the West itself benefited."

Dr. Maurice Bucaille
(*The Bible, The Qur'an and Science*, p19)
The high print-runs of this book earned the author
the 'Golden Book Award' for 1986

"If this be Islam, do we not all live in Islam?"

Thomas Carlyle (Scotland)
(*On Heroes and Hero-worship and the Heroic in History*, p 291)

Napoleon Bonaparte states:

"I hope the time is not far off when I shall be able to unite all the wise and educated men of all the countries and establish a uniform religion based on the principles of the Qur'an, which alone are true and which alone can lead men to happiness".

*(Bonaparte et l'Islam*, by Cherfils, Paris, France, p125)

Islam is indeed human nature. Let us see what Allah says in the Noble Qur'an:

**"So set your face firmly towards the Deen, as a pure natural believer, Allah's natural pattern on which He made mankind. There is no changing Allah's creation. That is the true Deen – but most people do not know." (Surah 30:30)**

As turned out by the creative hand of Allah, man is innocent, pure, true, free, inclined to right and virtue, and endowed with true understanding about his own position in the Universe and about Allah's goodness, wisdom and power. That is his true nature. But man is caught in the meshes of custom, superstition, selfish desire and false teaching. This may make man pugnacious, unclean, false, slavish, hankering after what is wrong or forbidden, and deflected from the love of his fellow men and the pure worship of the one true God. The problem before every prophet was to cure this crookedness, and to restore human nature to what it should be by the will of Allah, the nature on which Allah has created mankind.

So man deserves to live in peace and prosperity if he is within his own nature, Islam.

# Glossary

Here are some of the Arabic Islamic or Qur'anic words used in this book, translated into English with a brief explanation.

akhirah: the next world, what is on the other side of death, including the rising from the dead, the reckoning, and eternal life in the Fire or the Garden.

ayat: literally 'a sign', a verse of the Qur'an, also a miracle.

deen: life-transaction, religion in the broadest sense. The deen of Islam is *fitrah* – the natural condition.

dunya: this world, not as a cosmic phenomenon, but as experienced.

fitrah: the nature of a creation or a creature, i.e. the creature's natural condition.

iman: belief, faith, acceptance in the heart of Allah and His Messenger (SAAS).

jinn: inhabitants of the heavens and the earth made of smokeless fire who are usually invisible.

kafir, pl. kafirun/kuffar: the people of kufr (see below).

kufr: to disbelieve, to cover over the truth, to reject any of the articles of iman; i.e. to reject belief in Allah, His Angels, any of His Messengers, His revealed Books, the Day of Rising from the dead, and the Decree of Destiny.

mumin, pl. muminun: the people of iman (see above).

mushrikun: the people of shirk (see below)

qadi: a muslim judge.

ruh: the soul, vital spirit.

sadaqah: voluntary charitable giving for the sake of Allah.

shari'ah: what is laid down, the law of Islam.

shirk: the unforgivable wrong action of worshipping someone or something other than Allah, or of ascribing to someone or something attributes which belong to Allah alone.

shaytan: a devil, particularly Iblis who was one of the jinn, but there are human shaytans also.

Sunnah: the practice of the Prophet Muhammad (SAAS) and of his successor khulafa who took the right way, particularly that of it intended as the practice of Islam.

taqwa: awe or fear of Allah which leads a person to obey Him and avoid disobeying Him.

tawhid: the Islamic science of the unity of Allah and His attributes.

ummah: the entire community or nation of Islam.

English equivalents of Arabic names mentioned in the Qur'an.

Ibrahim (Abraham), 'Isa (Jesus), Jibril (Gabriel), Isma'il (Ishmael), Ishaq (Isaac), Musa (Moses), Nuh (Noah), Ya'qub (Jacob), Yunus (Jonah).